NEW
LAND
IC

Discovering
New Territory
and Finding
Renewal in
God

ANDREAS BOPPART

MONARCH
BOOKS

Published by
Lion Hudson Limited
Wilkinson House, Jordan Hill Business Park
Banbury Road, Oxford OX2 8DR, England
www.lionhudson.com

ISBN 978 0 85721 955 8
eISBN 978 0 85721 956 5

First published in German as *Neuländisch*, © 2018 SCM Hänssler im SCM-Verlag GmbH und Co. KG, Witten

First English language ebook edition 2018 Campus für Christus/Agape Europe
This updated English language edition 2020 Lion Hudson Limited

Acknowledgments

Text translation by Tracy Christman-König

Scripture quotations marked CEV are taken from the Contemporary English Version New Testament © 1991, 1992, 1995 by American Bible Society, Used with permission.

Scripture quotations marked ESV are taken from The Holy Bible, English Standard Version® (ESV®) copyright © 2001 by Crossway, a publishing ministry of Good News Publishers. All rights reserved.

Scripture quotations marked MEV are taken from the Modern English Version. Copyright © 2014 by Military Bible Association. Used by permission. All rights reserved.

Scripture quotations marked NIV are taken from the Holy Bible, New International Version Anglicized. Copyright © 1979, 1984, 2011 Biblica, formerly International Bible Society. Used by permission of Hodder & Stoughton Ltd, an Hachette UK company. All rights reserved. "NIV" is a registered trademark of Biblica. UK trademark number 1448790.

Scripture quotations marked TPT are from The Passion Translation®. Copyright © 2017, 2018 by Passion & Fire Ministries, Inc. Used by permission. All rights reserved. ThePassionTranslation.com.

A catalogue record for this book is available from the British Library

Printed and bound in the UK, February 2020, LH26

Hugs of gratitude go to Tamara, my four girls, Angi and Joni,
Peter, Silke, and Tracy.
Without all of you, there would not be very much of
Newlandic to read at all.
May the content of the following pages,
written by the sweat of my brow,
stir you up inside, excite you,
make you think, challenge you,
inspire you, move you,
and perhaps make you sweat from time to time as well.
But, most of all, may these words awaken a desire for
New Land inside you, too.

"Andreas 'Boppi' Boppart is a remarkable leader with passion for prayer, evangelization, and unity within the body of Christ. He brings a powerful message of hope for the church in Europe and a bold and inspiring witness to the good news of Jesus Christ."

Nicky Gumbel
Pioneer of the Alpha Course and
Vicar of Holy Trinity Brompton, London

"While politically our continent is falling back from unity to old divisions, spiritually a contrary movement is taking place. Christians are moving together from old divisions to a new unity in Christ. Andreas Boppart is a great gift from God in this field, unifying Christians from all different backgrounds so that the world can see Christ. He is leading thousands to Jesus and closer to the heart of God, both in the Protestant and Catholic world."

Fr Raniero Cantalamessa
Preacher to the Papal Household

CON
TENTS

Foreword by Pete Greig

On 13 October 2016, a giant silverback gorilla called Kumbuka escaped from his enclosure at London Zoo. The media went crazy with the story as images of King Kong marauding through New York City flashed through the public consciousness.

But the reality was a little less exciting. Kumbuka merely broke into the zookeeper's kitchen. He sat down to drink five litres of sweet, undiluted Ribena, was recaptured, sedated, and returned to his enclosure to recover from the mother of all sugar hangovers.

The apostle Paul says that "it is for freedom that Christ has set us free" (Galatians 5:1, NIV). We have been liberated from the cages of sin to embark upon great adventures with and for Jesus Christ. But many of us squander our freedom. We play it safe. We get distracted by childish cravings. We hang around familiar cages. We drink blackcurrant squash in the zookeeper's kitchen when we could be climbing the Empire State Building!

My friend Andreas "Boppi" Boppart is more like King Kong than Kumbuka. He is a big, bold, wild guy, taking risks, inspiring thousands of people to embark upon the greatest adventure of them all.

In *Newlandic*, Boppi calls us to explore new lands, to learn new languages, and to live life to the full. I found myself inspired once again by Boppi's passion to live with greater courage, not ashamed by the gospel but taking my stand as a citizen of heaven on earth. I also found myself equipped by this message, to make big changes in lots of small, simple, practical ways that anyone can do.

Whether you are new to the Christian faith, or have been a believer for many years, this book will inspire and equip you to return to the heart of discipleship. Let's put down the Ribena, break out of the zoo, and take our cities by storm!

Pete Greig
International Director, 24–7 Prayer,
Senior Pastor, Emmaus Rd, Guildford, UK

FANTASTIC

Introduction

" That's one small step for man, one giant leap for mankind."
On 21 July 1969, Neil Armstrong spoke these words as
he became the first person ever to set foot on the Moon. You
might like to think that this important step has nothing to do
with you, but then you would be completely wrong. Space
travel precipitated an unbelievably long list of discoveries
and developments that directly or indirectly affect our daily
lives: memory foam, enriched baby formula, clear braces,
in-ear thermometers, scratch-resistant sunglasses, battery-
powered tools, smoke detectors, precise GPS systems, digital
image sensors for cameras, improvements in plane design,
aerodynamic design for lorries, damping systems for buildings
and bridges, and an international rescue system, among others.[1]

What would life be like if people in previous generations had
never ventured into New Land? More than just spices would be
missing from our kitchens without explorers and adventurers.
Almost all of life's comforts would disappear. We stand on the
shoulders of pioneers of the past, and now it is our turn to enter
New Land.

I generally see people developing in two main directions in
their spiritual lives: either they become better as they go through
life, or they become bitter. I am inspired by all those who grow
deeply in their faith with an open heart and develop a sort
of "elderly generosity", or sense of serenity and composure. A
"Newlandic spirit" echoes within them as they go through life
continually conquering new territory. And yes, I've made up the
word "Newlandic". Throughout the book when I use this word,
know that I mean an attitude that is constantly seeking to move
forward into New Land with God. It's an attitude of openness,
adventure, and obedience. But at the end of the day, the New

Land spirit is much more. It is waiting to be discovered, defined for you as you walk with God.

It makes us uneasy to think that God will never be finished with us or with our faith. He designed life as an adventure to be discovered as we follow Jesus and walk into the New Land that God has prepared for us.

Faith does not belong in a perfectly square box that you keep tucked away, unopened until the end of your life; instead, it must be free to develop and evolve.

More than ever, our world needs courageous people who actively seek the kind of faith that continues to deepen: people who do not just have a vague belief, but who follow Jesus with their whole heart; people who do not dwell in the past, but instead look forward, orientated toward the "Newlandic" way of thinking, acting, feeling, and believing in a way that affects their own lives and is contagious to those around them. The purpose of "Newlandic" is to stimulate dulled curiosity and invigorate dead desires.

I started writing this book in the Graubünden region of Switzerland, where I lived for many years, and I finished it here in Zurich, where we never wanted to live. God led us here, though. Part of me still mourns the move, but mostly I am full of anticipation for whatever God has prepared for us in this new place. Because whatever he prepares for us is always good. It may not be easy or comfortable, but it is always good and right.

And because it feels so right, I am filled with that well-known and sought-after "inner peace". I'm right in the middle of New Land. Despite the tingling sense of apprehension, I am exactly where I want to be, where I belong. Because it feeds my Newlandic spirit. Are you ready to make a move? Ready to enter New Land? "Life is either a daring adventure or nothing at all." That's how the deaf–blind author Helen Keller described it. Your adventure awaits!

MUSCLE MASS

A universal principle for living things is that if something does not move, it will eventually die. The heart reminds us of this with every beat. I recently stumbled upon a story online about an ascetic guru from India who has been holding his right arm up in the air for years. Over time the limb died, and now he cannot move it anymore.[2] If something does not move, it will eventually die. When a system is balanced (and that is exactly what biological systems naturally strive for) and the molecules no longer move around, death is certain – at least biologically speaking. We, too, need to stay in motion, always moving forward. You can choose to stop breathing, eating, or drinking, but it won't be long before your body gives up. In the same way, our faith and spirit will wither if we stop moving forward. German politician Gustav Heinemann said, "Those who refuse to change will ultimately lose what they seek to preserve." The first result of standing still is losing what you had in the first place.

Our brains also need to be exercised and continually fed with new information. If those cells are not stimulated, they will cease to perform at the same level and instead decompose. The good news, though, is that with the right kind of stimulation, the human brain can recover and expand, even after being damaged. It is preprogrammed to keep learning – throughout a lifetime. If we stop using it, our mental faculties decline. Use it or lose it![3]

My kids inherited a ride-on wooden toy cow from their great-grandmother. This family heirloom has been passed down through the generations for more than a century. This little cow is in amazing condition – you can see that it was hardly ever played with, probably because everyone realized that it was so valuable. My kids just loved that toy, but they did not just want to look at it. They could not wait to ride around on it. As a result, after only one week, it had lost one of the feet and its bell was missing, too. I'm not sure which was more frustrating: the thought that in just a few hours my kids had managed to destroy a toy that had survived for more than one hundred years, or the fact that such a great toy had hardly been played with for so long because everyone thought it was too valuable to use. We should not make the same mistake with our minds. The brain is not a museum piece, something meant to stay in mint condition, locked away in a cupboard and unused. Instead, the mind stays sharp because it gets used regularly. When I say "used", I mean that it continues to learn and try new things – even with regard to faith. If we fail to use our faith over weeks or months, then the "faith muscle" will begin to atrophy. This is why it is essential that we use, exercise, and build up our faith continually. This happens automatically when we step into New Land. When we intentionally put ourselves in new and challenging situations, we realize our need for God's help. The ancient mystic Saint Teresa of Ávila said it like this: "I believe that it is impossible for love to remain still. Those who do not grow will wither."

This idea of growth is based on a biblical principle found in Matthew 25:14–30. Jesus tells a story about a man who went on a long journey and entrusted different sums of money to three of his servants, based on their ability to manage them ("silver talents"). Two of them increased their money in his absence, but one buried his talent in the ground in order to ensure that he could return the full amount when the boss returned. The boss praised the two who made more money, but he called the third "wicked" and "lazy" and even took the talent away from him.

Jesus is talking about talents as a specific measure of weight, but ultimately we can use this story to think about whatever possessions and talents God has given us. These could be our abilities as well as our personal charisma or even our faith. When we fail to make use of the personal assets God has entrusted to us, when we do not invest them wisely so that they multiply, then we are thwarting our purpose in life. We are in danger of losing whatever we are trying so hard to preserve.

Many Christians refuse to move into spiritual New Land because either they think that faith is unchanging, something that is imposed upon them in a specific form, or maybe they are secretly afraid of what the Unknown could do to their faith. New Land can certainly shake our foundation and force us to rethink some of our most basic beliefs, to question things and sort through everything again. Out of fear of uncertain and even uncomfortable situations, people often begin to block out anything that is different, foreign, or new, which results in them achieving exactly what they wanted to avoid: the wasting away, or even the death, of their faith.

If you want to keep your faith alive, you can't bury it and let it suffocate. You have to invest in it and allow it to multiply. This happens when you intentionally put yourself in places and situations that force you to depend on God completely, and when you surround yourself with people who are fundamentally different from you and whose walk with Jesus looks completely different from your own. This is the best chance you have to experience God in new ways. Only in the strange and inconvenient places can you discover new, previously unknown aspects of God's character. This will broaden your faith, without causing you to worry too much about what you might lose in the process. The benefits far outweigh the risks.

When was the last time you stepped into New Land? How have you done this in the past few weeks or months? Think of a time when you discovered or learned something new. Take a few moments to answer these three questions and describe what you learned specifically about:

1. yourself,
2. other people, and
3. God.

Even if you couldn't answer these questions, keep reading. Or if you had lots of answers, keep going. It's worthwhile to continue on this journey. Just walking on the path will bring you into New Land; a traveller never returns home the same.

New Land changes people.

TERRA INCOGNITA

If we are not ready to enter New Land, we risk giving up the ground that has already been claimed. If we stand still and stop investing in our relationship with God, we will soon find it difficult to manage life's changes – at church, in our personal lives, and in relationships with other people. If we are not connected to the source of "living water", we cannot give water to others and growth is impossible. People around us dry up, wither, and become bitter – and so do we.

The Bible talks about lots of people who stop moving forward in faith. Think about the scribes, who refused to let go of their traditional understanding of God and faith. Or the rich young man who had a passive sort of faith and kept all the commandments – until Jesus challenged him to let go of things that were dear to him and to come and follow him. The man walked away sad; he didn't really want to move forward spiritually (Matthew 19:16–26).

This kind of response is often preceded by frustration, disappointment, or hurt that has not been worked through completely. Instead, we begin to build walls to protect us from getting frustrated, disappointed, or hurt again. This interrupts an important – and perhaps uncomfortable – inner process of healing that would drive us into God's arms.

Maybe you'd really like to enter into New Land, but you are disillusioned. You have tried and failed time and time again. Or perhaps you've just had enough of all the empty promises of amazing things that will happen if you just believe more, pray harder, or fast longer. In the end, nothing happens. Don't worry: I'm not trying to pull you into something that doesn't exist. And it's really not about just doing "more". Instead, it's all about establishing a Newlandic spirit in our lives and faith. I want to encourage you to take action as you sense God leading you into something he has prepared. Don't be discouraged by negative experiences from the past or become idle.

Maybe you think that everything about faith has already been discovered and there is nothing new for you to find. You could easily say that adventure is no longer possible in the twenty-first century. I am jealous of those ancient mariners and explorers who set off into the great Unknown, who had so much "Terra Incognita" ahead of them. That term was used on old maps to describe areas that were still unexplored and unmapped.

In fact, there is still more uncharted territory today, far greater than what has already been discovered. The more we know, the less we understand – the riddle keeps getting bigger. How does the brain work? What is a black hole? Where or what is the soul? No one knows the answers to these questions. The universe is one huge question mark, and it is presumed that about 90 per cent of galaxies are as yet undiscovered. Although twelve people have been to the Moon, only three have been to the deepest part of the ocean – the Mariana Trench. By 2011, we had identified about 1.3 million species on earth, but experts estimate there are around 8.7 million left to be discovered (give or take about 1.3 million).[4] The number of undiscovered sea creatures is estimated to be far greater than the number of land animals we have as yet discovered. Huge areas of the Sahara, the Arctic, and the Antarctic have only been photographed by satellites. There are still large areas in the Amazon rainforest, the Congo, and Papua New Guinea where no explorer has ever set foot. Although all the highest summits (over 8,000 m) in the Himalayas have been reached, there are still a few 6,000 m peaks just waiting to be climbed.

Even if there are no more areas marked "Terra Incognita" on today's maps, the Unknown still exists and is waiting to be discovered. You don't even have to make a huge physical effort, since the most exciting Terra Incognita is not somewhere out there, but exists inside you. Because God lives in us, there is always something new to discover. After all, he is the one who creates New Land within us and who is waiting for us to take that first step to explore further.

The Terra Incognita inside you is not unknown to God at all – he is already there; after all, he is the one who created it. So it is essential that you open yourself to God and discover what he created in you. If you get to know God, you end up getting to know yourself.

This book is meant to encourage you to release your inner explorer or adventurer and to set out on the journey that God has planned for you. You can find out who he is, who you can be, and what Terra Incognita he has prepared for you so that you can conquer it together. This God of the New Land wants to challenge us, mould us, and lead us to new shores again and again.

I hope that you experience something similar to what I feel when I step into New Land with God at my side: fears are blown away, my faith becomes deeper, and I am liberated. All of a sudden I can breathe a bit more freely, like inhaling pure Swiss mountain air as I wake up in a cabin on a mountainside in my home in Graubünden after having spent decades only breathing in big-city smog. Give God a chance to develop your inner New Land and to deepen your faith.

1

MOR PHIC

The New Land God

I am not God. That alone should fill you with relief and hope. But at least I am a little bit like God. That is true for you, too. Although a lot of that In-God's-Image stuff carries an air of arrogance and can easily be confused with thinking you are God, I'm talking about something different. Since we are made in God's image, it is absolutely essential that we know who God is and how he thinks, feels, and works. Just think, we probably have some of those same qualities in us. Jesus said, "If you have seen me, you have seen the Father" (John 14:9, CEV). If we want to know what God is like, then we need to look at his Son.

One of God's main characteristics is that he is always looking for New Land. He moved into New Land with Jesus Christ in a big way – by becoming human, for one example. God's love for newness is reflected in nature: in the changing seasons that are all about making everything new. However, it is not about throwing away the old to make room for something completely new; instead, God makes the old new again. He invented recycling.

If you want to follow Jesus, you will inevitably enter New Land. If you don't want to go there, then you will end up going around in circles. But the same is undeniably true for you and for me: regardless of where we are right now, God has prepared New Land for us. He is intrinsically Newlandic and he will always point us in the direction of New Land so that we keep moving forward.

GOD SPEAKS NEWLANDIC

Because God's character is Newlandic, he also speaks the language. It is worthwhile for each of us to figure out what that means for our lives. Lots of misunderstandings in life stem from the fact that we fail to realize God speaks Newlandic and that he always leads us into new areas of our lives so that we discover more and more about who we really are.

He plants our feet squarely on New Land, or brings us to a "broad place", as the Psalmist says in Psalm 31:8 (TPT). Constant renewal is God's strategy for every person's life. He loves to bring renewal; in the Bible, our future is described with the words "I am making everything new" (Revelation 21:5, CEV), and that future begins today. Colossians 3:10 (CEV) says that we are new people who are becoming "more and more like… [our] Creator". This renewal process lasts a lifetime and happens daily.

You are a citizen of God's New Land. That was determined before you came to be. This citizenship carries with it the implicit challenge to discover the new person you are and to strive for transformation, because God wants to continually mould you and stretch you. I have come to see this as the most important way that I perceive God's presence in my life: by acknowledging his transformational power in me.

I have personally experienced God changing my hardened heart, and this is the biggest miracle I can imagine. I am probably still not the most compassionate man who shows empathy by breaking out in tears when people share stories of personal suffering. Recently, somebody approached me at a train station wanting to talk and asked me to pray for him. He stubbornly ignored my protests of "Well, now is not the best time", and dived headlong into his distressing life story. He missed all my obvious signals to make him stop. I had a headache, was so hungry I could've screamed, and I didn't want to listen to or pray for anybody.

It took a full twenty minutes and an apathetic, mumbled prayer before I could flee to the nearest bench, desperate and frantic with hunger, where I hid until my train was ready to leave. Maybe God had something in mind with that encounter – after all, I had only met the man because I just missed the earlier train and had an hour to kill before the next one. I am not always ready for what God is doing, and in moments like those, the Old Boppi has his hands firmly around the throat of the New Boppi, choking him until he turns blue and faints on the floor.

Despite the fact that I refused that particular invitation to enter New Land, God has been able to change me over the years, and my heart of stone has become a lot softer. He planted a new spirit in me, and it is being renewed daily (see Ezekiel 36:26). It's a process. And that's exactly how it should be. God creates his Newlandic spirit in me and points my heart toward whatever new territory he wants to show me on a particular day. This is what Romans 12:2 is talking about, too:

> *Don't be like the people of this world, but let God change the way you think. Then you will know how to do everything that is good and pleasing to him.*
> (CEV)

I have fallen in love with this verse. First, it describes the renewal of our thinking into what God intends. This is how we grow into a new thought culture shaped by heaven. When we allow this to happen, when we "let God change the way we think", this transformation takes place in us. Being transformed means growing into what God has called us to be and do. It is a wonderfully beneficial and even pleasant process, especially since we are so tempted to bring about change ourselves by force. That way, we let things become strenuous, dogmatic, and overly pious.

Second, I really love the phrase "everything that is good and pleasing to him". I have started basing all my decisions on this principle. When faced with a decision at work, we now start by asking as a team the question, "Do you think that would be pleasing to God?" Almost every time, we are able to find consensus by reaching out to God, looking for his way rather than trying to find the path that pleases us (although our own desires are always involved to some extent). Somehow, making decisions in this way strikes a chord deep within; it just feels good, and it brings peace. Depending on the topic, this process may include agonizing debate, but even difficult decisions produce that positive feeling of peace when they are based on our seeking what will please God.

In my opinion, one of the biggest pitfalls for Christians is that we stop allowing ourselves to be renewed. Either subconsciously or consciously, we become convinced that we are "done". We start to think that we have figured out how everything works and what the point really is. We believe our faith and our perception of the world are now complete. This is a dangerous fallacy that makes us arrogant toward people who have experienced God in a different way and immediately stops us from becoming more like Christ. "Anyone who thinks he is someone has stopped becoming someone" is how Socrates put it.

In my youth, I was convinced that the Christian faith is something static (although I didn't realize that I believed this). This subconscious belief affected my relationships and the way I interacted with people. My thinking was inflexible, and I often got into arguments with people who held different beliefs or had a different worldview from my own. I basically thought that at some point everyone should have figured out how God fitted into their worldview and how they should adjust their worldview to accommodate God. I knew exactly what the perfect moral life should look like. Consequently, I also knew who wasn't living right. But a person's faith is anything but static and finished, something that you cook until it's done, store in a plastic bag, and leave in the freezer for the next few decades or so. The Swiss army has something we call "Atomic Bread" – it is made to survive a nuclear attack, to still be edible when everything else has been destroyed – even twenty years later.

The problem with this static impression of faith is the personal conviction that we have been stranded on the Island of Truth, and anyone who thinks or believes something else is on the wrong island. We become unable to enter into an honest dialogue because we become more interested in convincing than listening. Faith is a process. It grows along with us and changes through the years. God will not be finished with us at a specific point so that we can take a seat on the nearest bench and wait until life comes to an end. Instead, he leads us into New Land again and again.

Entering into faith is not like going to the cinema, where you take your seat and watch the same film over and over for the rest of your life.

Faith changes over time, in the same way as things that we believe are important or that we hold to be true. Not all truth is absolute – some things are only true for a particular phase of life. For example, for my three-year-old daughter, the current truth is that she is not allowed to play on the road. This makes sense because it is potentially dangerous for her, although very few cars drive down our street. When she is older, this truth will be adjusted: "Be careful when you walk down the road." Later on, we'll take the next step and play football on the road together.

Of course, this cannot be directly applied to faith in every case, but this concept would have helped me in my teenage years to understand how ideas or beliefs can be limited to a certain time. Today, however, I experience God calling me out of those self-imposed and seemingly clear limitations more often, to go outside the "fences" (see Psalm 18:19).

GOD LOVES LOOKING THROUGH NEW GLASSES

One characteristic of God's Newlandic being is his fondness for shifting the paradigm, often to challenge us. Sometimes we forget that everything we assume to be real is merely the version of reality that we perceive through the lens of our own personal glasses. These glasses are our history, our experiences, our ideas, our desires, etc. A paradigm shift means a change of our usual perception and mindset. It brings a sudden change to how we experience reality and the challenge to think and act differently. In the past, it has always happened to me when I have taken a step out of my comfort zone, beyond familiar boundaries, and then turned back to look over my shoulder meekly and reflect on my life to date.

The Bible proves that God not only allows paradigm shifts in our lives, but he actually brings them about. The prime examples are the incarnation, the resurrection, and the outpouring of the Holy Spirit. My friend and office partner, Peter Höhn, has this to say:

Sometimes life is like an earthquake: everything that seemed right goes awry. Your previous worldview doesn't fit anymore, and you're forced to see reality differently than before. The Bible shows us that God loves to broaden people's horizons in this way.

This can happen through radical and surprising experiences that send us into the world, at times against our will, through natural life processes or even through voluntary decisions like marriage, having children, or a career change.

Of course, God is faithful and reliable. He reveals himself in the Bible as the one who remains eternally constant. Yet, at the same time, he is the one who makes things new (see Isaiah 65:17), who intervenes in our plans time and time again, who breaks through our walls to go forward with us so that we may understand his bigger plan. He speaks into our lives to move us into new territory.

The renewal of our minds is essential for us to mature spiritually as followers of Jesus. This is why God directs us into situations that cause us to rethink important, even fundamental issues. It is good for us to hold on to important qualities like loyalty, stability, and a focus on our life's purpose, but, at the same time, we ought not to latch on to rigid concepts that make us hard or cynical. It's like that little rubber washer in a water tap that keeps it from dripping. It has to stay stable and remain in place, but it must also be flexible, pliable. If it becomes hard and brittle, the tap will begin to drip. I don't mean to say that someone with an inflexible personality has got a screw (or a washer) loose... but it is true that new thinking is not always easy.

We spent three months in the Philippines, and during that time we had to make some changes as a family – regarding everything from culture to temperature. Once we got back to Switzerland, the adaptation process started all over again. When one of my daughters was sitting on the toilet, she was annoyed because she didn't know where to throw the toilet paper anymore. In the Philippines, she had learned that it belongs in the little bin next to the toilet. (If you throw it in the toilet, it clogs the pipes.) She was also sceptical about drinking tap water at first, because we had drilled the idea of "diarrhoea water" into her. We have to adjust to new situations over and over again in life; what used to matter is no longer valid, or it moves into the background because it doesn't apply to our current life situation. Some things may even become inappropriate or wrong.

It is definitely helpful to view crises and conflicts in life as chances, as entry gates into a new phase of life, and opportunities to shift the paradigm and renew our thinking – even if the process is sometimes unpleasant and painful.

Think of a time when God used a situation to challenge you to renew your thinking and to accept change.

God has communicated with me in Newlandic ways in various areas of my life, my thinking, and my faith over the years. It seems to me that he takes great joy in encouraging us to get new glasses. So, if we want to know what God is planning, we need to learn to understand the way he speaks. And then we need to go along with him, to follow where he has gone before us. It's not New Land for him, and it should reassure us to know that we never walk into the Unknown alone because we have the best possible tour guide at our side.

GOD'S NEW LAND NEVER ENDS

Because God is Newlandic and you and I are born of him, we are also citizens of New Land. You may be empathetic, artistic, apathetic or stoic, a lyric, a cynic, a little exotic and erotic, you might even be majestic or eccentric, but most of all, you are Newlandic.

There are people who just reek of adventure, sort of like how I stink of sweat after a battle on the tennis court. Ernst Tanner, founder of the Swiss Helicopter Mission (Helimission), is that kind of pioneer and living legend that you usually only read about in books. He told me the story of when he became the first person to cross the Sahara by helicopter. However, that spectacular adventure almost never happened because on the way to Africa, within ten minutes after take-off, he had got so off course that he had to land next to a restaurant somewhere between Bern and Geneva to ask for directions.

I admire Ernst, his son Simon, and the other Helimission pilots who help people in need, often under unimaginably difficult circumstances. They have all experienced unbelievable things like emergency landings, ambushes, shots fired at the aircraft, and even crash landings due to inclement weather when they were trying to reach the last remaining cannibal tribe in the heart of the Papua New Guinea jungle.

I, on the other hand, was never the kind of daredevil child who had to test every limit. While others defended their territory by beating one another over the head with little buckets and spades in the sandpit, I was usually on the receiving end of their blows. When real men are looking for a testosterone fix, like Bear Grylls digging maggots out of a camel cadaver in the wilds of the desert or sucking the liquid out of cows' eyes to survive, I'm just sitting on my sofa, munching on a bag of crisps and sipping my ice-cold energy drink. But I have realized that even I – the ultimate average joe – have a slumbering urge for adventure. When I was young, after I had watched a film with friends about a group of people who survived a plane crash in the mountains by eating the flesh of dead passengers, we all had a taste for adventure. I can't remember how everything came together or how we came up with the plan, but I found myself with two friends in a field in our local cemetery as we set ourselves up to spend the night outdoors under a military tarp as snow began to fall. We didn't sleep much. I kept trying to tell myself that the man-eating whatever-it-was would start nibbling on the kid at the other end of the row first, giving me that crucial head start for my getaway sprint.

I am convinced that an adventurer lives inside you, too; for, regardless of your personal need for safety, you are a citizen of New Land. From the moment you began to exist, you were either condemned or called (the choice is yours) to be an explorer. "Life is change, and without renewal, it is incomprehensible," said the Russian philosopher Nikolai Berdyaev.

I have been able to observe this drive to explore in my four daughters from their early years. From birth, they have done nothing else but explore and discover the world. Regardless of whether they approach it with fear and trembling or with daring courage, they already have great journeys of exploration behind them, including giant mishaps and tests like "finger versus hob" and "scissors versus lower lip".

If we follow Jesus, he will automatically lead us into New Land. He goes before us; we follow behind. This process of discovery does not end with our death and the transfer into eternal life. Ephesians 2:6–7 states it clearly:

> **God raised us from death to life with Christ Jesus, and he has given us a place beside Christ in heaven. God did this so that in the future world he could show how truly good and kind he is to us because of what Christ Jesus has done.**
> (CEV)

The word "done" is interesting – other versions translate it as "show",[5] "demonstrate", "illustrate", or "uncover". William MacDonald also writes:

"Heaven will be our school and God our teacher. 'His grace' will be the subject and we will be the students. And the school year will last for all eternity. This should free us from the expectation that we will know everything when we get to heaven. Only God knows all things, and we will never be completely like Him."[6]

MacDonald assumes that we will never know all there is to know about grace and that God will continue to reveal things to us throughout eternity.

The same word, *endeiknumi* ("to show"), is also used in 2 Timothy 4:14:

> **Alexander the metalworker did me a great deal of harm. The Lord will repay him for what he has done.**
> (NIV)

Instead of "done", this verse uses "did me harm". The sense of "show" has been replaced by "to experience completely". This also applies to the previous verse. "Experiencing completely" does not happen in an instant, nor is it complete upon our arrival in heaven; instead, it continues.

Through the ages, God will show us what his grace is all about. One eon is not enough to discover the immeasurable wealth of his grace. Only an eternity of ages will be enough time to begin to develop, unfold, and open up the immense and incomprehensible grace of God. Therefore, in Lamentations 3:22–23 we read:

> *Because of the Lord's great love we are not consumed, for his compassions never fail. They are new every morning; great is your faithfulness.*
> (NIV)

You cannot treat God like a picture, sit down in front of him, and look at him until you have explored every little detail. At some point, even the most fascinating image does not reveal anything more, because you have searched and studied every square centimetre a dozen times. But God is not a picture. He reveals himself to us in his essence every day and that will never end.

You will never be able to fully fathom his grace, his mercy, his love, his faithfulness, his truth, or his goodness. Paul writes in Ephesians 3:19 (CEV), "I want you to know all about Christ's love, although it is too wonderful to be measured. Then your lives will be filled with all that God is." This is also about that ongoing process, discovering "more and more" who God is, how he operates, and what it really means to live of him.

We are learners, and we always will be. To me, this is a fascinating statement about an eternity that sounds anything but boring. That's the place you were always intended to be. That's where you belong. Here on earth you have a specific nationality.

You live in this world right now, but you have been adopted into another. You could say that you have been granted dual citizenship. You belong in New Land! So my primary identity is neither Swiss nor European, but I am, first and foremost, a citizen of New Land.

How will you live in light of this awareness of your Newlandic citizenship?

2

PANIC

Fear of the New

It is completely normal to be afraid sometimes. It is also normal to be fearful of new things. But when we are moving forward – and not just in circles – into the New Land that God has prepared for us, then we have to learn to look our fear in the eye and to overcome it, with God's help.

Living in fear, welcoming our anxieties like guests into our home, keeps us from having the life that God intends for us.

Fear blasts holes in our faith just like I used to shatter my sister's Smurf toys with my BB gun. They didn't survive the attack, and our faith will similarly end up with lots of dents and chips. Ultimately, we take our eyes off the goal and end up missing out on the beautiful land that has been granted to us from heaven. All the Israelites who stood at the edge of the Promised Land and chose to believe the lies of the spies instead of God missed the New Land promise out of fear. God had told them about it in advance: this is "the land I am giving you" (see Numbers 13:2, CEV). "There is good land, rich with milk and honey" (see Exodus 3:8, CEV). If they had only trusted, everything would have been fine. But instead of believing God's promise, they allowed their fear of giants and of looming defeat to determine their response and overcome them completely. Only Joshua and Caleb held on to God's promise. And only those two were allowed to enter the Promised Land in the end, while the rest of the Israelites over twenty years old had to do a few extra laps in the desert, ultimately dying there.

The greatest enemy we have to overcome in the process of conquering New Land is our own fear. As long as we are walking around on the earth and have not reached eternity, where God's presence will surround everything and permeate us, fear will pop up like that nasty last flake in my cereal bowl that evades the aim of my spoon each time. The problem with fear is that it doesn't just sit there passively; instead, it stays below the radar, influencing your life in whatever way it can.

Fear always causes us to make bad decisions and will take you down the wrong path every time. Fear is the reason you wrestle with doubts, certain feelings, and thoughts in secret instead of sharing them with your partner or your friends. Fear is why you work like an animal that is being whipped to go faster and faster and, in the process, you shirk your responsibilities, ignore relationships, or miss out on time with your family. Fear is why you associate with the same type of person over and over again, or maybe not at all. It is why you always say "no" or "yes" and why you might believe more falsehoods than truths in some areas.

Huge segments of our society are affected by fear, saturated with it like a soaked sponge, and it oozes out of our media everywhere. Ultimately, our fellowship in the kingdom of God is also often affected by fear, and worries about our own little kingdoms impede many blessings. However, fear is not a characteristic of Newlandic culture. It is perhaps the number one obstacle to blessing. This is why it is so important to uncover our own fears and anxieties that suck the life out of our souls like a leech and become the unseen drivers that influence our decisions.

When I am faced with an important decision, I always ask myself, "Why?" Why do I have the feeling that this situation needs to be resolved in this particular way? If I realize that fear has crept into the equation at some point, then I bring the worry to light – that usually does the trick. I can remember specific decisions in which I only recognized the fear factor after the fact – and I only remember them because some of those choices required long and painful processes to set things right again. Don't let fear take the wheel and drive your life.

THE SOCK-EATING MONSTER

Just last night, my four-year-old crept into our bedroom with the excuse that she couldn't sleep because she was afraid. I remember what it was like as a child to be convinced that some nasty, evil shadow on my wall had begun to move. Before I went to sleep, I was always careful to check under the bed – just to make sure the hungry sock-eating monster wasn't lurking there, waiting for the chance to nibble on my duvet or visit the sock drawer buffet. Next, I spent what felt like a good hour huddled under the covers, willing myself to sleep, often only with mild success, because I ended up dripping with sweat from being wrapped up in all the blankets. At some point I stumbled across the ultimate anti-monster strategy: turning the lights on solved the problem instantly and calmed the raging seas of my young soul.

Fear of monsters under the bed is now, three decades later, thankfully no big deal anymore – on the one hand, you grow out of it, but, on the other hand, our mattress sits on wooden pallets very low to the floor. Only really small monsters would be able to fit under my bed now, and they don't usually make too much trouble during the night.

Unlike most monsters, some fears and anxieties don't just disappear as we grow older. It depends on your personality and the kinds of experiences you have had in life. Some fears only develop as we grow older: fear of being alone, fear of flying, fear of getting an illness, fear of pain, fear of being abandoned, fear of death, fear of failure, fear of rejection, and many more.

The list is endless, just like all the medical terms people have created to name every possible form of fear (and the nearly impossible ones, too). For example, arachibutyrophobia is the fear of having peanut butter stick to the roof of your mouth.

Bargainophobia is the fear of sales, a form of anxiety that I, as a man, have no trouble imagining when I picture tables overflowing with sale items and an aura of hysteria hanging in the air. According to statistics, one of the most prevalent forms of anxiety is the fear of public speaking. This often ranks higher than the fear of death.

I have no idea what your nightmares are made of. Lots of my anxieties have to do with food – the fear of a sour rhubarb cake or a soggy puff pastry shell with mushrooms. There have also been phases in my life when I regularly felt anxious about dying when I lay in my bed at night. First, my chest would tighten, then my thoughts would start to circle around different death scenarios like vultures circling over carrion. I was only able to scare the vultures away by thinking up elaborate distractions in my head. But this only helped for a short time. At some point I started talking to Jesus about it. Our fears are in good hands with him.

In fact, fear has an important purpose. It is not wrong to be afraid. For example, being afraid of fire ensures that we don't play around with it. Fear of falling from a height reminds us to be careful and protects us from unnecessary injury. Many anxieties are healthy and keep us safe in life. Sometimes they give us a necessary shot of adrenaline to deal with a difficult situation. But fear becomes problematic and counterproductive when it stops protecting or empowering us and begins to paralyse and block us. This is exactly the point where we need to learn how to enter into a New Land and culture without fear.

What are your greatest fears? Fear of failing a test, of spending your life alone, or of losing an important relationship? Perhaps fear of death or of a terror attack? Are you worried about an economic crisis – or about anything that feels different and uncomfortable to you?

Perhaps you are afraid of becoming ill or the fact that there is usually too much month left at the end of your money? Do you wonder whether your faith will really deliver on all the promises in the end? Are you afraid of the future? Maybe you are afraid of God and the New Land he has planned for you?

Sometimes we are haunted by the misconception that, as a Christians, we are no longer afraid or allowed to be afraid. This is completely false. Jesus said that it is normal to be afraid as long as we are in this world (see John 16:33). At the same time, he offers us a place to bring our fears – to him directly. He wants to show us the light switch.

THE ANTI-FEAR SWITCH

When we were living in the Philippines as a family with young children, my fears accumulated rapidly. Typhoons, rebel troops, cockroach attacks, endless flights with four small children, mosquitos carrying dengue fever, sinking ferries, poisonous water snakes – and, in fact, many of these fears were legitimate. We did come face to face with poisonous water snakes when we went swimming, and a typhoon passed over our island shortly after we arrived there. The storm buried villages that we had visited under metres of rocks and mud and removed roofs of homes we had slept in. That experience helped me realize in a new, deeper way that these fears cannot protect me from anything at all – they only create obstacles that hinder me in life.

I can choose whether I want to give in to fear, which will make me unhappy, or whether I want to turn to Jesus, the one who conquers fear, and allow him to show me the light switch in that particular place of fear. When I get nervous on a plane, I find it helpful to distract myself. But with deeper fears, trying to distract yourself is like trying to hold a buoy under water. No matter how hard you try to push them down, they just keep popping up to the surface. This is why it is so important to stop avoiding fear and face it head on. These are the moments when I pray my shortest prayer, "Jesus." That has become my light-switch word. It really makes a difference for me, and the stormy seas of my soul become calmer.

Prayer gives us the opportunity to come close to God's heart and to soak up his love for us. This love is what drives out all fear. The Bible says, "There is no fear in love. But perfect love drives out fear" (1 John 4:18, NIV). Where God is present, so is his perfect love. And then there is no place for fear – just like in my childhood bedroom, when the monster had to flee as soon as I turned on the light.

We are born of God, so we come from a place ruled by pure light. But we have been born into a world in which God is no longer present in a way that permeates everything; a world in which fear has taken root and spread. We come from a No-Fear Zone, and we are moving toward a future that includes a return to the presence of God, a return to the No-Fear Zone. In the meantime, though, our lives take place in the here and now. This means that we will have to deal with fear. Fear is the absence of God. It is not something that we naturally know, but something that life teaches us.

Just like darkness is the absence of light, fear is the absence of God's love in specific areas of our lives. Whenever fear stirs in me, it means that I have not given God enough space in that particular area of my life, that I have not immersed myself in his love, and that I am not acting out of love. It shows me that I have not yet found the light switch in that particular room of my heart, or maybe the dimmer switch is just turned down too low. It is a simple spiritual principle that the opposite of God's love cannot simply be not being loved. Instead, it is fear. Wherever you have stuffed in as much of God's love as possible, there is just no more room for fear. This applies to everything that God is: if you take God out of the picture, things like hope, light, direction, truth, life, and love also have to go. All that remains is hopelessness, darkness, a lack of direction, lies, death, and a whole lot of fear.

I have been able to find my light switch in a few areas. People often ask me whether I get nervous speaking in front of thousands of people. A few years ago, God took me through an intense process that helped me realize who I am in him. Through that process, the idea that in everything I do, I want to please him alone – and not people – became deeply rooted in my heart. This thought freed me completely from stage fright – the fear of failing or being rejected by all those people, or the fear of facing a gaping hole of nothingness in myself. I am no longer afraid of these things, because I know that God loves me no matter what – even in the midst of the biggest failure I can imagine. And that is enough. I have found the light switch in the dark room of my stage fright. As long as I know that God is pleased with me and with what I do and say, then it really shouldn't matter what other people think.

Fear is like trying to drive with a flat tyre. You just don't get very far – you are blocked, paralysed, and things get damaged in the process. A flat tyre is the absence of air – just as fear is the absence of the Spirit. Recently, after I got a flat tyre, my mechanic sold me a new kind of tyre filled with foam. Now, if I drive over a nail, nothing will happen, because the foam immediately fills the hole so that no air is lost. In the end, it is not enough to be filled with God's love. We also need to make sure that his love stays inside us and that we don't have a leak in the system.

**What do you give yourself over to: fear or God's Spirit?
How much space do you allow God's Spirit to fill in
the different areas of your life? Where do you have a
spiritual leak that's allowing God's love to escape?**

I have discovered that biblical truth is like that foam in my tyre. When I hold on to God's promises, it helps keep God's Spirit from leaking out of my system.

**What kinds of strategies do you use to overcome fear?
Have you discovered your own light switch? What is
the special foam that keeps you from getting a flat tyre?
How can you flick the light switch when you realize that
fear is taking over?**

DISGUSTING TOOTHPASTE

If you are not exactly sure what fears are hindering you, then listen to yourself when you pray. Your ears should perk up whenever you hear one of those infamous "But God" prayers. They go something like this: "God, I'm ready to invest my whole life for you, but only if you keep hair from growing on my toes!" They often start with a "yes" to God, a readiness to do something, quickly followed by the "but" that reveals the underlying fear.

The things that come out in prayer reveal what is really in your heart. It's like a lemon – when you squeeze it, sour juice comes out. But it's not because of the pressure; what comes out is sour because lemon juice is just sour. In the same way, you are not just fearful or unloving or lacking faith because you have come under pressure in life. That fear, lack of love, or faithlessness comes out because it was already in you.

I catch myself praying those "But God" prayers every so often. "I will go wherever you want me to, God – but not to Africa." "I'm ready to do everything for you, God, but I don't want to preach." "You can have my life, but I don't want to be a missionary." "I'm prepared to move away from my hometown, but I don't want to live in Zurich." Interestingly enough, with each of these prayers, things turned out exactly as I didn't want them to. So, I can tell you: be careful when you add a "but" to your prayers. Each of those unwanted experiences was much better than I had imagined, and they blessed me richly. My first trip to Africa transformed my faith and brought me into a real discipleship relationship with Jesus. I have now been a preacher for more than half my life, and there is truly nothing else I would rather do. I am the national leader of a missionary association and I love it. I recently moved into the Zurich area, and it feels right – from my head down to my hairy toes.

When I am afraid that God wants to lead me into something or somewhere that I don't want to be, then a kind of fundamental mistrust rises up that he doesn't want the best for me – regardless of whether the new place will actually be unpleasant or not. The "buts" reveal my fears, and these can be traced back to a specific point: I do not trust God or his love. I do not believe that God wants the best for me.

These "but" anxieties hinder change and keep me from moving into new things. The "fainting goats" have a similar problem. I have often laughed at YouTube videos of this amusing species of goat. As a result of a genetic defect called *myotonia congenita*, these goats faint in the face of any perceived danger. Their protruding eyes make them look like they are terrified all the time anyway, just waiting for the next wolf roaming around in the bushes, or some kind of mountain man who likes to run through the herd screaming for the sheer fun of it. In these moments, the goats freeze, or they may even fall over, their gangly legs stiffly pointing upward. Their skeletal muscles all contract at once and stay that way for about ten seconds. For the goats, it is certainly an unpleasant quality – but they are now recommended as protection animals for sheep herds. If a wolf threatens the sheep, the goats would react and faint and become a gambit – like in chess.

When we give in to fear, the same thing happens in our brains. Our ability to think rationally is blocked, as if our brain muscles contract and make thinking impossible. We start choosing to do things that we don't really want to do, and, ultimately, we can become victims of that situation. New and unknown things often provoke a similar shock reaction in our lives.

Fear of New Land cannot be easily explained from a psychological perspective, but spiritually speaking, it's very clear. Because when God leads us into New Land, it is always good for us, although that good may very well be accompanied by discomfort and pain.

> *Lord, I have chosen you alone as my inheritance. You are my prize, my pleasure, and my portion. I leave my destiny and its timing in your hands. Your pleasant path leads me to pleasant places. I'm overwhelmed by the privileges that come with following you, for you have given me the best!*
> (Psalm 16:5–6, TPT)

"You have given me the best!" I have spent a lot of time in recent years thinking about the depth of this verse. Earlier in my life it was far too easy to blurt out how good God is. This opinion comes under fire when life deals us a difficult hand or when we go through tough times. It requires an act of will to work through those naive ideas and get past the brokenness so that we can get to a higher level of godly naivety – a place where we can truly say that God is good through and through.

> *Every good and perfect gift comes down from the Father who created all the lights in the heavens. He is always the same and never makes dark shadows by changing.*
> (James 1:17, CEV)

Whatever God gives us is truly good. More than that, it is perfect. This is why we never need to fear the New Land that God opens up for us.

We are all beneficiaries of the fact that people in the past have taken bold steps into New Land. All technical discoveries are thanks to those pioneers, even the little things that make our lives easier. I went to the Greek island of Kos on holiday once, to the place where Hippocrates drank his ouzo some 2,400 years ago. He is credited with defining medicine as a science, and he revolutionized dental care by developing a mixture of roasted mouse heads, cooked dogs' teeth, goats' ankle bones, chopped mint leaves, and white wine as toothpaste. I know you let out a sigh of relief, too, when you read the words "mint" and "white wine". Actually, I think it's pretty great that people like Hippocrates took steps into New Land and developed ideas like this. This was the beginning of today's dental care products. But I still don't want to know everything that is in my toothpaste… The American composer and author John Cage said, "I don't understand why people are frightened of new ideas. I'm frightened of the old ones."[7] We should not let our fear of the new hinder us and impede our personal development. This is even more important when the New Land comes from God, even if it sometimes leads us through storms.

A BIBLICAL THRILLER

The path into New Land with God is an adventure and does not always take us out of the path of the storm. But you don't have to have been born with a courageous spirit since, as actress Dorothy Bernard once said, "Courage is fear that has said its prayers." God wants us to discover him in the eye of the storm, our No-Fear Zone.

Once I had the opportunity to go on a cruise and lead church services as the ship's pastor. The route from Germany to Iceland via Scotland was full of ups and downs, although it was nothing like a real storm, as the ship's crew assured me. But when the sea was wild and the waves a little too high for my liking, I felt like a sock in a washing machine even when I was lying in my bed. The mere fact that my head and feet spent many a night going up and down like a see-saw produced an underlying nausea that kept me awake. But our waves were nothing in comparison to the storm the disciples experienced on the fateful day described in Mark 4–5.

That story just oozes fear and panic. I like to call it the Bible's horror film. It reminds me of a movie I got roped into watching once. My friends dragged me along, but I had no idea that the film we were going to see was a psychothriller.

I started to figure it out when a screeching violin began to play and that sound kept coming back throughout the film. From the top of my head, down my spine to my big toe, every hair was standing on end. That horrible sound went through my bones, and even when nothing happened, I was tied up in knots and tense all over. The fact that I was sitting in the front row, unnaturally close to the images, didn't help my frightened soul one bit. As I left the cinema, I realized that my lower arm muscles hurt because I had been digging my fingers into the armrests the whole time.

The soul has different strings, like a harp, that vibrate based on the situation we are in. During that film, my panic string had been plucked without doubt, and this is exactly what the disciples experienced too – to the extent that this point in their discipleship journey has gone down in history.

Everything began quite harmlessly that day, until Jesus announced, "Let's cross over to the other side of the lake" (see Mark 4:35, TPT). The "let's" was probably an exaggeration since none of the disciples would have been excited about the idea. The reason was the storm that was obviously brewing in the sky. Any local fisherman would have known that a crossing would be difficult that day. In fact, they sailed right into the middle of the storm. It was so powerful that even the weathered fishermen feared for their lives. This is the kind of situation in which you start writing goodbye messages in your head – just in case. Or at least they would have wanted to tell Jesus, "I told you so!" If they had had Twitter back then, maybe they would have used some of these hashtags: #greenintheface #hangingovertherailing #feedingthefish #ihatewater #goodbyecruelworld

Then Jesus, who was sleeping peacefully on a cushion even in the midst of the storm, stood up and commanded the lake, "Hush! Calm down!" The storm subsided and everything was calm. That must have been one of those moments when you feel a holy fear of God.

"So, they arrived at the other side of the lake, at the region of the Gerasenes…" the story continues in Mark 5. I like this unspectacular sentence. I imagine someone starting to tell the story with the word "so". It is not hard to imagine how much a word like that really meant. They had been so buffeted by the storm, they were so exhausted, they were still so unsettled, so confused, so wet, so seasick… But if you think the disciples had survived the storm, you are mistaken. Another storm was already on the horizon.

Jesus had hardly stepped out of the boat when a man, who was possessed by an evil spirit, ran up to him. The look on that man's face would probably have struck fear into the heart of even the most robust fisherman. If the disciples hadn't already wet their pants, they certainly had after that encounter. You may think I'm exaggerating, but think about this: according to Luke's Gospel, the man was completely naked. He lived in burial caves, was completely wild, and had superhuman strength. People had tried to bind him with chains, which he easily tore off. He was dangerous and he and another possessed man terrorized the entire region, to the extent that certain roads were no longer passable. He spent every day in the caves or on the mountains, letting out blood-curdling screams and pummelling himself with stones. The man must have been covered with swollen lumps, was bloody, and probably had broken bones or other disfigurements. An image that nightmares are made of – just like my horror film of years ago.

Since that part of the lake is about 8 km across, and a human scream is audible from up to 10 km away, the man's screams were probably an ominous messenger to the disciples. The joy of surviving the storm and reaching the shore passed quickly. When Jesus announced they were travelling to the other shore, none of the disciples was interested in getting any closer to whatever awaited them on the other side.

The possessed man fell directly at Jesus' feet and the demon in him cried out, "Leave me alone, Jesus, Son of the Most High God! Swear in God's name that you won't torture me!" Then Jesus asked his name.

"My name is Legion" was his unsettling answer. A Roman legion had about 6,000 men. So I can imagine that even robust

Peter's mouth was agape when he heard that. Jesus commanded the spirits to leave the man, and, at their own suggestion, he sent them into a herd of pigs that was grazing on a nearby hillside. It must have been quite a spectacle since the 2,000 pigs ran off the end of the cliff and plunged into the lake – probably accompanied by a cacophony of squeals. I can almost hear the whispered surrender, "I can't take any more!" as the disciples' faces grew pale once again. I bet that even Judas was distracted from calculating the value of all those pigs or considering an alternative solution to the problem.

The swineherds fled into the city and the towns, as Matthew describes, and a huge crowd formed to come and see what had happened. When they got to Jesus, they could hardly believe their eyes: the man who had terrorized the entire region for years was sitting next to Jesus, clothed and perfectly sane.

What an amazing miracle! I am moved by the thought of the transformational, healing power that we see in this story.

Something that surprises me, though, is the phenomenon of "After the Fear is Before the Fear". When Jesus stilled the storm, the disciples didn't burst into rejoicing. No; instead, the Bible says "they were more afraid than ever". The same thing happened to the people from the region where the possessed man lived. They had been terrorized by him for a long time, but when Jesus solved the problem and the man was sitting as gentle as a lamb, they were afraid then, too, and asked Jesus to leave the area.

This is a human reaction that I often observe. We are more afraid of change than of the uncomfortable or even life-threatening situation we are in. We have more anxiety about something new that God is offering us than about the horrible circumstances we are currently in.

I meet people all the time who long for change in their lives, who are thirsty for a God-encounter, but who are unable to let go and allow God to change them. They are afraid of what God will do to them or through them. Fear of looking at the truth, or as Uli Eggers, a friend and pastor, said, "For many people, suffering in their current situation is easier to manage and more comfortable than summoning up the courage to face the truth."[8] We are often more afraid of the good things that God wants to give us – albeit sometimes through wild storms – than of the bad situation we are currently in.

What change in your life are you secretly afraid of? Where do you need to cry out, "Hush! Calm down!" and invite Jesus into your stormy situation?

THE NO-FEAR ZONE

One other thing becomes clear in this stormy story. Everybody is afraid, from the disciples to the townspeople, from the swineherds to the possessed man. All the central characters of the story are afraid. Except Jesus. Not of the storm, nor of the crazy ranting of a possessed man, nor of a quick chat with a legion of demons. Jesus is free of fear. Even when everything around you is stormy and falling apart, the seas around Jesus are calm. He is the place to go with your fear, the place where storms calm down. So, there are only two options in life: live in fear or live close to Jesus. God's presence creates a No-Fear Zone. Or, as it is described in Psalm 89:9 (CEV), "You rule the roaring sea and calm its waves."

The closer we walk with God, our heavenly Father, the less we will fear a particular situation or something different, new, or foreign. I observe something similar in my children. On their own, they are usually too afraid to pet an animal, but if I lead them by the hand, they follow gladly in my footsteps wherever I go. Last winter, my second oldest was enrolled in skiing lessons. The first day was horrible. She couldn't understand the instructor, the atmosphere was chaotic with all the kids running around, and none of the instructors seemed to have the faintest idea of how to teach anybody anything. It nearly broke my heart. She didn't want to ski at all because she was afraid. Five days later everything looked completely different. We were always the last ones to come in from the slopes, and my daughter didn't want to stop. How was such a drastic change possible? I took her with me for an hour each day. She held on to my poles and we skied until her fear was gone. Having Dad by your side makes the difference – as a child, you are not usually afraid when your dad is around. It works the same way with faith. "You, Lord, are the light that keeps me safe. I am not afraid of anyone. You protect me, and I have no fears" (Psalm 27:1, CEV).

Despite staying near, God doesn't just blow all of life's storms away for us. Even when we pray for it. It is often better to be on the lookout for the No-Fear Zone, the eye of the storm where Jesus is, and then to stay close to him there. Storms are also able to shake us up, to point us in a new and better direction, to uncover things that have been buried in the past – and to open up the path into New Land. In the face of strong headwinds, it is your choice whether to build protective walls or windmills.

How do you navigate into calm seas during the storms of everyday life? How can you find refuge in the eye of the storm when the daily chaos threatens to overwhelm you,

you feel so vulnerable, and everything seems dangerous? (This could apply especially to parents.) How do you manage not to react in an angry way in a meeting when you disagree with everything and it all seems unfair? What is your strategy for running into the eye of the storm, your escape mechanism to dive headlong into the No-Fear Zone?

Fear limits the space we have to live in and turns faith into something that feels mechanical because you have subjected yourself to it. Instead of flying free, as in the No-Fear Zone, you feel like you have been squeezed into a little box, just like a cuckoo in a cuckoo clock. My grandmother had one, and I loved to watch it. Four times per hour that little bird popped out and presented his mechanical "cuckoo", then he disappeared back into his box. There was no hint of freedom and flight, far more a rote repetition of a song learned long ago just before running back into hiding. Lots of people live like that cuckoo, and fear is their little wooden box. Instead of flying free, they only look out every so often, as they try to keep some religious rules to the letter. Sometimes, if you watch them closely, you may find yourself asking, "How in the world did I get here?"

God did not give you a spirit of fear (Romans 8:15). Don't stay in your Fear Box. Although it may seem cosy and safe, at the end of the day, it can only limit you, hem you in, and become increasingly constrained. Do not be ruled by your fears. Look for your No-Fear Zone and flick the light switch on. For heaven's sake, fly! You weren't made for anything less.

3

ELAS TIC

The Expander

God often leads us through the narrow way of fears and storms in order to bring us to a broad place. Broad places are a prime characteristic of Newlandic culture that stretch everything we know: our understanding of God and ourselves, our heart, and our identity. A broader perspective also makes a difference in how you see other people – those who are different to you or who believe different things – and the world you live in.

I have come to recognize broad places and broad thinking as key to a mature and fruitful life of faith. It is also an essential quality for true cooperation among Christians. This is why moving into broad places with God has become one of my favourite themes, something very close to my heart. Living, believing, thinking, and acting with a Newlandic spirit is the complete opposite of narrow-mindedness. Being a citizen of New Land means broadening your horizons.

Either we get bogged down in our fears, worries, and philosophies of life or we allow God to lead us to broad places. That last one is exactly the direction he intends for our healthy development. But the sobering reality is that many Christians miss the path to God's open spaces because they reach an impasse at some point in their walk of faith. Maybe they have been lulled into a certain way of thinking by the spirit of this age, and now they are convinced that everything worth discovering has already been discovered, so there couldn't possibly be anything new to learn about who God is or who I am or how the world works. Lots of people simply believe that faith is something fixed and unchanging, like a pair of trousers you put on as a child, expecting they will somehow fit for your entire life. Nothing could be further from the truth. That kind of thinking is dangerous because it leads to narrow-mindedness.

It expresses itself in self-loathing, a critical spirit, prejudice, or even condemning other people's faith. You feel it when you are around people like this, that tightening around your own heart. This is the exact opposite of the redemptive and liberating effect that the gospel is meant to have.

Be honest:

Where have you discovered signs of "narrow" thinking or faith in your life? Where is God gently but clearly pointing his finger when you ask him?

As you are looking for narrow patches in yourself, it may be helpful to complete the following sentences as you think of specific people:

**I can't stand it when he/she...
It really bothers me that he/she...
I can see the mistakes in his/her faith in these areas...**

When you have formulated your answers, bring them to God in prayer. Where are these statements simply an expression of your narrow-minded, human soul and a narrow faith?

Where do you sense God calling you to have a broader perspective?

THE GECKO PHENOMENON

"But the Lord was my support. He brought me out into a spacious place…" (Psalm 18:18b–19a, NIV). These two inconspicuous sentences have become dear to my heart. At first glance, they seem to be an unlikely pair – something that gives me support will also bring me to a new, spacious place. Also, the German word translated as "support" in English denotes something solid, a firm foothold, a handrail you can hold on to when walking up a steep path, something that is fixed in one place and will not give way. Imagine an anchor; if it has been thrown into the sea, it makes it difficult to head out into open water.

When I was in the Philippines, I learned an unexpected lesson on this subject. Each evening, as I sat at home listening to the hypnotic hum of the mosquito zapper, I watched nimble geckos dance across the walls. They even managed to hang on when completely upside down. (Well, they usually managed to hang on… But whenever they did fall, it was always directly onto my wife, Tamara. She must be some kind of gecko magnet.)

A billion tiny hairs on each foot allow them to scamper around on the walls with great agility. (Those poor critters. The few hairs on my toes are already too much for me.) And then the light went on for me: these geckos don't just live on the ground; they can effortlessly reach all kinds of places. They have access to a new dimension, an open space. This is only possible because they are able to hold on. Those little hairs that give them support do not hinder them or slow them down; instead, they broaden their horizons significantly. It works in the same way for us when we find our support in Christ and not in things. When he is our anchor, then life is not fixed or rigid as some people think, but it is elastic, free, broad, and limitless. That kind of support makes anything possible.

We assemble our own fake anchors out of doubt and mistrust, trying to be our own support, and usually realize only too late (or maybe never) that these things hold us back instead of empowering us to move forward. A pseudo-anchor could be confidence in our own abilities or in our bank account (if you are Swiss), in our theological knowledge, or in a pastor. We make our own substitute Christs. Even limitations through fears may seem like a kind of support. If we are afraid that God wants to limit us or rein us in, then we can be tricked into believing that our own substitutes will give us the security we crave.

Where do you look for support and stability in your life? What things cause you to think, "Thank God I have…?" You have to let go of one thing to take hold of the right thing.

Sometimes our narrow-mindedness is revealed in negative thinking toward others. "How can that person call himself/herself a Christian and believe that?" "What they believe is completely idiotic!" "If that's how he lives, he mustn't know Jesus." It doesn't really matter what other people believe or do; it is our own thinking that has become narrow. Our hearts have no more space for self-reflection and self-awareness, love for our neighbour, and acceptance of others. We come to believe that only what we think is true and condemn anything that doesn't match our own thoughts, ideas, or beliefs. "Thinking is hard. That's why most people just judge," said Swiss psychologist Carl Gustav Jung.[9]

Christ wants to lead you to a spacious place and be your anchor at the same time. The phrase "to bring out" used in Psalm 18:19 is the same phrase used in the Bible to describe how God brought the Israelites out of slavery in Egypt. God always leads us out of the old and into something new, out of oppression into freedom, out of the unknown into a promise.

"To bring out" also has to do with salvation. The name Jesus, "Yeshua (ישוע)", means salvation, deliverance, and help and comes from the root word "yasha (ישע)", which means help or save. Jesus saves you by bringing you to a spacious place. Another possible origin of the meaning of the word "yasha" is "to be open, wide, or free".[10] So Jesus even carries this broad space in his name. Fascinating. He is the Saviour, the Healer, the one who leads us to broad places. What a comforting perspective and an example of God reaching out to us personally to lead us out of our narrowness into his spacious place, New Land.

Just as Jesus stretched out his arms on the cross to save us, now he stretches our hearts to make more space. When Jesus hung on the cross, it was not a seemingly abstract act to obtain the forgiveness of sin. Through his death on that cross, he brought "space" into our lives – a wonderful Newlandic component that will permeate every aspect of our lives, if we let it. The risen Christ has become my anchor. I am rooted in him. When he comes to bring space to various areas of your life, then things will become wider, never narrower. It is the complete opposite of constricting, cramping, or clinging.

"He brought me out into a spacious place; he rescued me because he delighted in me" (2 Samuel 22:20, NIV). God really does delight in leading you to a spacious place.

In what areas are you ready to let God lead you to a spacious place? In what aspects is the transfer onto a wider, broader way long overdue? Where do you already feel the narrowness yourself? What topics or areas of life are getting harder and harder to manoeuvre? Where are you beginning to feel twinges of narrow-mindedness and heaviness?

If we feel burdened, then we are likely yoked to the wrong wagon – or we have allowed ourselves to be roped into something that is wrong for us. "For my yoke is easy and my burden is light" (Matthew 11:30, NIV). The closer we come to God, the lighter life becomes, the lighter the things in our thoughts, faith, and daily life become.

Paul writes to the Corinthians:

> *We have spoken freely to you, Corinthians, and opened wide our hearts to you. We are not withholding our affection from you, but you are withholding yours from us. As a fair exchange – I speak as to my children – open wide your hearts also.*
> (2 Corinthians 6:11–13, NIV)

Paul's heart was not always open – it had to be stretched by God. He writes in the previous chapter, "So from now on we regard no one from a worldly point of view. Though we once regarded Christ in this way, we do so no longer" (2 Corinthians 5:16, NIV).

Do not stay in the narrow place, and, most of all, do not let your heart become hardened and your thinking and faith become narrower over time. God has planned a very different process for you: the exact opposite. Faith should stretch us and broaden us; it should be something light and easy even in the face of difficult circumstances.

"You have not given me into the hands of the enemy but have set my feet in a spacious place" (Psalm 31:8, NIV).

Here's a suggestion: do an inner inventory – together with God – of the areas and topics in which you have a tendency toward narrowness. Then take yourself up to a high place – a mountaintop or a high tower – where you have a wide, panoramic view that makes it easy to dream big. If you don't have any mountains or towers nearby, then try putting a chair on top of your kitchen table and having a seat. Write these areas on a piece of paper and fold it into a paper plane; then send your plane flying and symbolically move into New Land in those areas you identified. While you're at it, shout out a liberating "yasha" as you watch it glide into the distance.

I cannot be responsible for any looks you might get from shocked passers-by, but I am sure that God will lead you to his spacious place when you invite him to do so.

THE PAPER PLANE MESSAGE

In 2011 a group of ambitious amateur scientists released 100 paper planes into the air from a height of 37 km somewhere over Germany. "Project Space Planes" had been launched by Samsung to show how robust their memory cards are. At that altitude, temperatures can reach -50° Celsius. The scientists researched the best design for the planes and used a weather balloon to take them up as high as possible until the valuable cargo was released. The paper planes, each one with its own memory card containing a personal message, took off somewhere over Wolfsburg in central Germany. The most amazing part was finding out where the planes finally landed: planes made it to Canada, the USA, Russia, India, South Africa, and even Australia – some 15,000 km away from the launch site. Normally, a paper plane will soar for a few metres at best – at least for me. You might even get it to go a couple of dozen metres, depending on the design you choose, your starting point, and whether or not the wind is on your side. One time, at an event, I made a bet with one of the musicians on stage with me to see whose paper plane would fly the farthest from the stage. My competitor threw his plane first, and it had to work hard to reach the fifth row. With a snort, I strode up to the launch spot, sure of my impending victory, and sent my plane off with a bit too much gusto. It did a loop-the-loop at first but then took a nosedive and landed just beyond the first row. You know, it's not that easy to throw one of those things well. Sometimes the conditions are not favourable for travelling far. It could be bad design, poor wind conditions, or just a botched throw.

You can sometimes look up to heaven and yell at God about the less than optimum conditions of your life that are holding you back from really flying. However, the interesting thing is that it doesn't really matter whether you are flying a robust Airbus or an ultra-light plane. The experiment with the paper planes in Germany shows that the most important factor in achieving long-distance flight is the height you start at. The principle is simple: if you want to go far, you need to start from as high a point as possible. The closer you are to heaven, the further you will fly; and that means you need to be as close to God as possible. It is your nearness to God that makes a long-distance flight possible. Your relationship to him – the intimacy you share with him – soaks into every area of your life, stretching you in the process. Although I only had one throw from the stage, most things in life are not as straightforward as a one-throw paper plane contest. But I live out of God's grace, thanks to which I can throw over and over again.

How close are you to God right now? What needs to change so that you can draw close to him, so that you can be close to heaven again?

God wants to stretch your thinking and your faith more and more. But we have to allow him to do it. In Isaiah it says, "Enlarge the place of your tent, stretch your tent curtains wide, do not hold back; lengthen your cords, strengthen your stakes" (Isaiah 54:2, NIV).

Pull up a couple of your tent pegs and move them back a bit further than before, tightening the ropes. And if you feel like crying out that this path is fraught with danger and that we have to tread carefully so that we don't get so wide that anything could happen, then you can relax. You are probably not in danger of landing "too wide". Most often these kinds of comments come from the very people who will never become too wide. Trust God and take bold steps with him to the broad places of New Land.

THE NEW LAND COMPASS

If you think of your life like a country, it has different directions, like a compass. We can look in these different directions and grow wider in each one. I would like to tell you about four

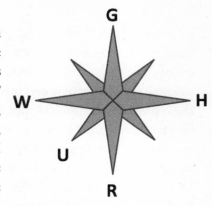

main directions that seem central to me, although there certainly could be others as well. These are: the "God" Territory, the "Heart" Territory, the "Relationship" Territory, and the "World" Territory. I also include "Unity" in the "Relationship" section, so there is a fifth point facing southwest.

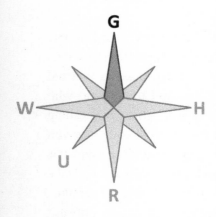

God Territory: More than anything, God wants to lead us to broad and spacious places, at least in terms of our awareness and experience of him. God himself is the prime example of New Land. Oswald Chambers wrote, "Never try to make your experience a principle for others, but allow God to be as creative and original with others as He is with you."[11]

What a powerful truth. We tend to draw conclusions about God based only on our personal experiences. Then, if somebody else has even a slightly different experience, we find it hard to understand or accept that as genuine. This approach neglects one important detail, namely that God was not made in our image but that we were made in his. It is not hard to imagine that I as one individual can only reflect a tiny part of his personality. So it should follow that God is reflected in completely different ways by other people. When I meet these different people, instead of being irritated because our experiences with God don't match up exactly, I can follow my curiosity on a voyage of discovery to get to know my God in new and different ways – in and through all those people. Sometimes we put God in a box simply by limiting him to the sum of our previous experiences, keeping him stuffed into our old boundaries of spiritual understanding. Along the way, we learn how he could be, and then we refuse to alter our image of him. And when we read the Bible, our personality glasses generally focus on one thing and read into the text based on our own way of thinking. But watch out – we need to keep our faith elastic.

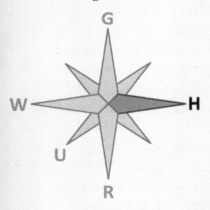

Heart Territory: God wants to bring your heart to a spacious place so that you discover yourself more deeply and understand who you really are, what your calling is, and what God intended for you when he made you. This is why it is essential for you to explore and take in as much New Land as possible. You can never begin an outward journey without having at least started on the inward journey.

Snakes have an amazing ability to shed their skin over and over again during their lives. They have to do this because they eventually begin to feel uncomfortable in their own skin; it gets too tight. So, from time to time, the old skin has to be cast off to make room for the new skin to emerge. For young reptiles, this happens monthly, and as they grow, it reduces to three times per year. If they didn't go through this process, snakes would end up like kernels of corn. When they are heated, the water inside expands. When it reaches about 200°C, the kernels explode (like popcorn). Snakes can be glad of two things: 1) that they don't grow that fast, and 2) that they can shed their skin.

Our "inner self" grows throughout our lifetime. We also need to shed our old skin and renew ourselves spiritually from time to time, otherwise things get a bit tight. One key aspect of the inward journey is to discover your own identity. This identity is inseparably linked to what God sees in us. As our Designer and Creator, he cannot help but love and be proud of us, although we may ask how that is possible given all our rough edges and the occasional sharp corner. It is because he generously overlooks our faults. Maybe this is similar to the phenomenon that economist Michael I. Norton discovered in 2009: the IKEA Effect. He theorized that people value an object that they have built themselves more than a mass-produced product. Similarly, when instant cake mixes appeared on the market in the 1950s, companies overcame the initial poor sales by emphasizing the importance of the housewife's contribution of eggs or a personalized decoration on the cake. After that, instant cake mixes were here to stay.

God must also have given in to the IKEA Effect. Through the grace he offers us in Christ, he is prepared to overlook our dirtiest stains. He loves us so much and places a much higher value on us than we give ourselves.

Relationship Territory: God wants to lead you to a spacious place in relation to your relationships with other

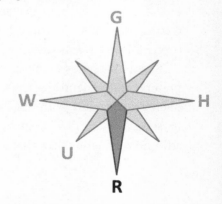

people so that you discover and realize who people really are and how God sees them. The key to healthy relationships is not focusing on what separates, what annoys, what fosters competition, or getting entangled in gruelling battles with people, but instead to see others as complementary, something that extends or completes us. This approach saves us a lot of time and energy and liberates us much more as we learn to serve one another with our strengths and balance out one another's weaknesses. This is why it is so important to explore and expand into Relationship Territory.

Unity Territory: One specific subsection of Relationship Territory is the topic of cooperation among Christians from different backgrounds and traditions. God wants to lead you to a new, broader place with regard to Christian unity – something 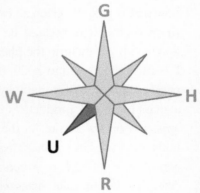 that we can experience today to an extent that was, until recently, unthinkable. It is about realizing that the war is over and that God creates a new dimension where a new type of cooperation is possible. He wants to show us the richness of his family.

Based on serious and usually well-meaning attempts to preserve and defend the truth at all costs, we Christians have often dealt harshly with our brothers and sisters in faith. This harshness or lack of love can become a cloak to hide an arrogant attitude, a haughty heart that lords things over others. A lack of love is a betrayal of faith. Jesus' greatest commandment in Mark 12:30 (CEV) is not "You must defend the truth with all your heart, soul, mind, and strength." Unfortunately, the following statement of Paul is often uncomfortably accurate, although said in a different context, "I know they love God, but they don't understand" (Romans 10:2, CEV). We attack everything that appears to stray from the truth, often fighting more to prove who is right than to preserve the truth.

But this fight is really about love, especially in relationships. I am not trying to diminish the importance of truth; it is a fundamental value we share. However, the greatest commandment was and is to love God, others, and ourselves – with all our heart, soul, mind, and strength. John adds:

> **But if we say we love God and don't love each other, we are liars. We cannot see God. So how can we love God, if we don't love the people we can see? The commandment that God has given us is: 'Love God and love each other!'**
> (1 John 4:20–21, CEV)

All our attempts to preserve the truth – at least whatever we believe to be the truth – have led to many wounds and hurt feelings, defamation of character, and ultimately to splits and separations among Christians. But we are supposed to accept one another as Christ accepts us (see Romans 15:7), although "accept" does not mean we have to agree with everything. No one is immune to being overly enthusiastic in their defence of a deeply held conviction and developing a lack of insight as a result. This fact should stretch our hearts toward others and make us more generous. As Christians, we need to keep in step with Jesus and follow the path to new, wide open spaces in the Newlandic culture.

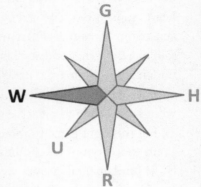

World Territory: God wants to lead you to wide open spaces with regard to our world so that you do not get entangled in the mixed-up mess of world issues and the protective shell of hope around your heart is not slowly scraped away like cheese on a grater. It is all about discovering a much broader scope for God's kingdom. Adding that new dimension to your thinking, seeing the world through God's eyes, and adjusting your horizon to perceive God's presence and working despite the confusion of politics and power in the world today are reasons why World Territory is important.

The following chapters will illustrate what it means to enter and possess these five territories of New Land. Everything is built on the foundation of getting to know God more deeply with every step you take.

4

EPIC

The God Territory

In 1985, John Cage wrote a piece for piano using a randomizer, which he adapted for organ two years later. It is entitled "ORGAN²/ASLSP".[12] ASLSP stands for "as slow as possible", an indication of how the piece is to be played. This is definitely a subjective instruction; so, at the world premiere, the piece lasted twenty-nine minutes.

At an organ symposium, some musicians came up with the idea to take that tempo indication a bit more literally. They decided to perform the piece in Halberstadt, Germany, the location of the oldest documented organ of the modern era. Because they would begin performing the piece in the year 2000 and the organ had existed for 639 years already, they determined that the piece should last for 639 years. They divided the eight pages of notes into segments lasting a total of 639 years, but they were delayed and the performance did not begin until 5 September 2001, so now the piece will last well into the year 2640. The end will be heard twenty-one generations after me, by my great-great-great-great-great-great-great-great-great-great-great-great-great-great-great-great-great-great-great-grandchildren. As the piece begins with a rest, the first note, an E, was heard on 5 February 2003. Since 5 October 2013, a D#, an A#, and another E have also been heard. The next note will be played on 5 September 2020 – seven years later. No one will be able to hear the entire piece. We can only ever be present for a small part of the whole.

It is the same with God. If he were a melody, we would never be able to hear his entire piece, not even in a whole lifetime. His timespan is so much longer than ours, and he is the only one who sees the complete picture. We will never come to the end of the piece entitled "God" and then start from the beginning all over again, like that irritating repetitive music you hear when you are on hold on the phone.

The "God" composition will not come to an end when you get to heaven, nor will it last 639 years. God's "as slow as possible" fills all eternity with music. What an epic concert! Nevertheless, sometimes we feel like we have already heard everything God has to offer, that the same melody and chords just keep repeating. But really, we haven't even finished the introduction yet. Or, to use another illustration, we haven't even touched the "train of his robe". Isaiah caught a glimpse of heaven and was completely unable to comprehend God's dimensions. So he mumbles something about how God's robe fills the Temple (Isaiah 6:1), and that is about all he can say. There is so much of God to discover that we should be glad he plays his melody "as slow as possible", otherwise we would be completely overwhelmed.

God is Newlandic par excellence. We will never be finished discovering him. We will never reach the boundaries of his personality. At the same time, though, we have the wonderful opportunity not only to learn about him, but also to know him personally in a relationship that grows deeper over time. Some things simply defy logic, and that is why we cannot keep God within the constraints of our own understanding. He is not bound by the limitations of our minds. We can learn how to believe beyond these boundaries. Make sure you intentionally plan times to explore and discover God's New Land. Everything in your life flows out of your relationship with God.

Do you allow God to renew, stretch, and add to your understanding of him on a daily basis? Maybe it's time for another dose of "daily renewal".

Go to your favourite place and sit down with God. Hold your heart up to him and let him reveal himself to you in a completely new way, or to show you a new aspect of himself that you don't know yet.

Ask him to plant something new in your heart.

THE SOUND OF "I LOVE YOU!"

Faith in God is not like a Polaroid photo that you take and then hang on the wall to let it turn yellow and eventually fade away. Our faith is constantly evolving as we discover new things about God. If we are not aware of this, then everything slowly becomes colourless and stiff; we become "holier than thou" and our hearts get puffed up. We start to tell others what is right and wrong – although this usually means we are telling them that we are right and they are wrong. It's a one-way street that ends in a cul-de-sac. Or we discredit others, questioning the genuineness of their faith. The constant stream of new discoveries is God's way of keeping our heart soft and flexible. If you want to stay spiritually young and dynamic, let God renew you daily.

It may be confusing to some to realize that your faith is more malleable than you think – or perhaps than you had hoped (if you are the kind of person who is looking for something hard and fast to hold on to). This is what happens when you have a natural affinity for clear structure or, like me, love lists and tables you can use to tick things off. But God didn't plan things that way. If we want to take him and his word seriously, we need to be aware of the fact that we naturally look at things through our own personal lens, a pair of glasses shaped by our life experience that we cannot simply take off at will.

God's truth, as I understand it, is always God's truth seen through my own personal lens and based on my current level of understanding. This is precisely why it is so important to have other people around us who show us a different perspective. Just as we do not walk through life wearing the first pair of shoes we ever got, our faith should eventually outgrow its initial form and develop with us over time.

One example of these changes is how the simple phrase "I love you!" in regard to God changes over the years – as it should and must. When I was a child, my "I love you!" was without questioning or even a shadow of a doubt. A couple of years later as a teenager, that same "I love you!" became a boisterous shout of courage that often came out without thinking and was sometimes pretty melodramatic. I jumped into wild missionary activities for Jesus and stayed up all night for him on several occasions. I had tears in my eyes when the realization of God's undeserved love swept over me. As a student, that simple, naive love came under attack, and my "I love you!" got a bit more cautious and reserved, but no less serious. When the first tragedies began to rain down on the lives of those around me, the "I love you!" became more like a question – I want to love you, but can I really? How close is your love to me? In times of failure, my "I love you!" was said through sobs and in the hope of being fully accepted. And in those "heaven meets earth" moments, my "I love you!" is filled with gratitude.

Every situation, every age, and every phase of life has its own "I love you!" that we need to seek and discover continually. It is not about discounting the "I love you!" of youth or trying feverishly to hold on to it. In fact, we need to regularly return to our first love, just as the Christians in Ephesus are challenged to do in Revelation 2. Even if it sounds slightly different from the first time, our love for God is always Newlandic and is always being reshaped.

How did Jesus' "I love you!" to his Father sound when he was fleeing Herod as a child? What about when he was a teenager? And when he got baptized and the Spirit came upon him? What did the "I love you!" sound like when Jesus turned water into wine? What about when he walked on water? Or when he wrestled with himself and God in the garden and asked for the bitter cup to pass him by? And then, when he realized that his best friends had fallen asleep at the moment he needed them most? What must that "I love you!" have been like when he hung on the cross? Or right after the resurrection?

God does not change; he is always the same. But we have the privilege of getting to know him more and more throughout our lives. So our "I love you!" should not be a reaction to the current situation, but simply a response to all that we see in God. We have to learn to adapt our "I love you!" to our knowledge of him, not to the circumstances of life at the given moment.

If our love for God becomes dependent upon circumstances, then it will quickly evaporate when things get tough – along with our discipleship and our worship. But that is not the idea; our love should not flow out of a steady stream of gifts from God or the fact that things are going well. Instead, our love for God is the only reasonable reaction to the fact that God is God. This is epic. It is often those difficult situations that drive us to start looking for God in earnest. That brings new shades to our "I love you!"

How does your "I love you!" sound right now? What "shade" is your love for God today?

THE BIG SECRET

A while ago, somewhere along the path to New Land, I stumbled over the word "secret" while reading my Bible. Paul uses it often in his letters. But one verse in the first chapter of the letter to the Colossians caught my attention. Paul talks about a "secret", which is always exciting. My kids love secrets, although they aren't so good at keeping them. Recently one came to her sister with a huge smile on her face and said, "You're getting a present. I'm not supposed to tell you what it is." Then, almost without taking a breath she added, "It's a princess book!" But secrets can also be painful when they are meant to hide something – for example, when you keep something from your partner.

But nothing spreads faster than a secret once it gets out. If you want something to get around to as many people as possible as quickly as possible, then just add in the caveat, "But remember, it's a secret." That way everybody will want to take the credit for telling their two or three best friends the news before anyone else hears it. It's a sign of trust. Revealing a secret is almost never a big surprise – it is often more surprising to discover that there is anyone around who didn't already know about it.

Basically, though, positive secrets are wonderful because they connect people. When Paul starts to tell us about a secret that was kept over generations but has now been revealed, everybody's ears perk up. And then good old, tight-lipped Paul drops the bomb, "And the mystery [secret] is that Christ lives in you, and he is your hope of sharing in God's glory" (Colossians 1:27, CEV). I love this statement and the massively deep truth that is stuck to it (like the chewing gum in my daughter's hair the other day). People ask me all the time, "What's so special about being a Christian?" "What's so different about life when you're a Christian?" Paul gives the answer right here: it is this added dimension of Christ living in us.

When you look at this in combination with verse 19, the full scope of this secret becomes clearer: "God himself was pleased to live fully in his Son." We have the Creator God with his full being in Christ and Christ in us. The full force of God's tremendous creation power lives in you.

Christ in us is our hope, and nothing or no one else: not your greatest efforts, nor your lovely smile, your perfect church attendance record, your astonishing level of giving, your ecological footprint, not even your eloquent prayer or the perfectly timed programme at your church. The one and only true hope is Christ in you. It is crazy to realize that the holy Creator God did not think it was beneath him to make his home within us. If that doesn't seem at least slightly odd to you, then you have already been dulled by Christian socialization.

What do people see when they look at you? What words would people use to describe your life?

Your hope is Christ in you! Think about how you can live your life in the most transparent way possible.

GOD'S JOURNEY TO MEET YOU

I have already written about how essential it is for us to always draw near to God. It is a relief to hear that God is always drawing near to us, too. One of his best qualities is that he behaves in diametric opposition to his creation. While the entire universe is expanding, God has decided over the course of world history to continually drift toward people. Since the colossal break at the Fall, which separated us from our intimate togetherness with God, he has been on a journey to bring us back to our original condition in order to be close to us again. In this pursuit, he has revealed himself in new ways time and time again. God remains the same, but he has shown himself to us in different forms.

I have described a couple of significant steps in the journey that God makes to be near to you and me. I know that this comparison is a little shaky, but the basic premise remains intact: that God has always drawn close to us, starting with the form he chose to come in. And it all began with his original idea – Paradise.

Tangibly close: First he was together with people in the Garden of Eden. "Late in the afternoon a breeze began to blow, and the man and woman heard the Lord God walking in the garden" (Genesis 3:8, CEV).

At a distance: Then, after the Fall, he was suddenly very far away. After that, he had to approach people more intentionally. "But the Lord came down to see the city and the tower the people were building" (Genesis 11:5, NIV). His love has always been greater, and he overcame the separation between us as the God who draws near.

Exclusively: God spoke through the Spirit to specific individuals. "Leave your country, your family, and your relatives and go to the land that I will show you" (Genesis 12:1, CEV). And this continues with the prophets, judges, kings, and other chosen individuals.

Signs and wonders: The fact that God acts through signs and wonders was and is still today a reminder of his presence and relevance to our situation. He makes himself directly available to us so that we can experience him. "There an angel of the Lord appeared to him from a burning bush. Moses saw that the bush was on fire, but it was not burning up" (Exodus 3:2, CEV).

A pillar of cloud and a pillar of fire: This would certainly have been a striking contrast for people who believed in a God who had previously only revealed himself to selected individuals. Suddenly they could see him as a pillar of cloud or fire going before them. "During the day the Lord went ahead of his people in a thick cloud, and during the night he went ahead of them in a flaming fire. That way the Lord could lead them at all times, whether day or night" (Exodus 13:21–22, CEV).

In the tabernacle/Ark of the Covenant: God no longer appeared as a mass of diffuse water droplets or flames, but he became approachable, although touching him remained forbidden. "I also want them to build a special place where I can live among my people" (Exodus 25:8, CEV).

In the Temple: When he had had enough of camping, God made his home in the Temple, but he was still not accessible to everyone. Still, people could localize God and "go to him". "I have chosen and consecrated this Temple so that my Name may be here for ever. My eyes and my heart will always be there" (2 Chronicles 7:16, NIV).

As a person: This had to be the biggest break of all: God, the untouchable and holy Creator, became human in Christ. "The Word became a human being and lived here with us" (John 1:14, CEV).

Spirit in us: All of a sudden, he poured out the Holy Spirit – and not just anywhere, but directly into us. The Holy God wants to live in us through his Spirit. "You surely know that your body is a temple where the Holy Spirit lives" (1 Corinthians 6:19, CEV).

With God: God's desire is to restore the uniquely deep intimacy that he originally intended to have with people. "Look! God's dwelling place is now among the people, and he will dwell with them. They will be his people, and God himself will be with them and be their God" (Revelation 21:3, NIV).

Looking at these examples, it is not hard to understand that people didn't always get it. Imagine if God revealed to us that from now on he would only live in and speak to us through animals. I would definitely not stay as cool as Balaam when his donkey struck up a conversation with him. It would take a lot of energy to change my image of God. It would be equally strange for us to talk to one of the Israelites who had wandered in the desert. She would tell us how she saw God every day — either as a pillar of cloud or fire. It would be so normal for her, and so irritating for you if you didn't know the Bible story. After all, you probably haven't experienced God very often as a pillar of fire that comes down into your front garden while you cut the grass.

God reveals himself to his people in new ways all the time. At one time he lived in the Temple, but if anybody entered the Holy of Holies without authorization, they had to die. Then, suddenly, the holy God became a man who walked the earth, farted occasionally, and a whole lot more that probably wouldn't fit into the traditional image of holiness. It is a tremendous notion that requires a lot of willpower and a large portion of Newlandic faith to digest.

Just like a shape-shifter, the unchanging God changed his form — not to be unpredictable, but in order to draw near to us. This is the epic journey of a loving Father returning to his children. To be near to us. This is what makes his idea to "live in us" so impressive. It is not possible to be any nearer to us and to our hearts than to live directly inside them. This is the highest form of intimacy, the greatest love proposal ever — a God who wants to be near us. He is a God who constantly moves into New Land in order to meet with us as a loving Father and to come into intimate fellowship with us.

Where have you discovered opportunities for intimacy with God? How do you experience God's nearness?

How close do you feel God is to you? How close do you allow him to come?

And how close would you like to come to him?

THE PATH OF ASAPH

It is essential that we figure out how to connect with this God inside us. I try to take little breaks throughout the day to "go inside myself " and spend time with him. I don't have to take a day off every week and hang out on top of a lonely mountain next to the cross mounted on the summit. Sometimes it's just enough to put everything aside for a moment, take a deep breath, and then look closely at what is going on inside myself. All I need is a little time to sort through that big pile of thoughts and feelings that occupy my mind – my thoughts to the left, God's to the right, mine left, God's right, and so on, and whatever I'm not sure about stays in the middle. When I take a timeout to visit God inside myself, I am often amazed at how even complex things suddenly become clear. But more often than not, the main result is that I feel calm and relaxed.

Asaph, one of the singers in David's court, had a similar experience. In Psalm 73, he describes a difficult situation that nearly caused him to "slip and lose his foothold". His heart begins to rumble. Next, all his thoughts and emotions boil over like milk on the hob. He starts getting jealous of people who are proud and godless, and he cannot understand why their lives are so easy. "From their callous hearts comes iniquity; their evil imaginations have no limits" (verse 7, NIV). They open their mouths wide with pride and slag off everybody around them for all they're worth. They even mock God – and still have no worries or money problems. Asaph can't quite seem to make sense of it all, and he ends up being tormented by these thoughts all day long.

I sometimes have situations that I can't let go of. I don't always find the exit out of that hamster wheel in my mind, causing sleepless hours during the night. Asaph is fighting a very normal battle, as it annoys us when we recognize that God's grace flows equally to both the good and the bad. "He causes his sun to rise on the evil and the good, and sends rain on the righteous and the unrighteous" (Matthew 5:45, NIV). But the concept only works as long as I have the feeling that I am on the Good Team.

It is all about our sense of justice, an inner compass deep inside. My kids are constantly checking to make sure they are getting as much as the other ones. As soon as one of the girls discovers that her sister has a square centimetre more meat in her sandwich, everything melts down. Naturally we don't favour any of the girls, but we also want to teach them that even if you don't always get exactly as much as everyone else, you can still be happy. But that begs the question: how can we expect them to understand what most adults still haven't figured out? Deep inside us, that primal cry for justice is always ready to leap out – although our understanding of justice does not 100 per cent match up with God's either.

But right in the middle of Psalm 73 a 180° turn takes place. The verses take on a completely different tone:

Yet I am always with you; you hold me by my right hand. You guide me with your counsel, and afterward you will take me into glory. Whom have I in heaven but you? And earth has nothing I desire besides you. My flesh and my heart may fail, but God is the strength of my heart and my portion forever. But as for me, it is good to be near God. I have made the Sovereign Lord my refuge; I will tell of all your deeds. (Psalm 73:23–26, 28, NIV)

The last verse includes the phrase "… as for me, it is good to be near God". How is Asaph able to change his tune now? It's as if someone flipped a switch. I found the key to this change in verses 16–17: "When I tried to understand all this, it troubled me deeply till I entered the sanctuary of God…"

Asaph did exactly the right thing in one of those dark moments when he couldn't see a way forward. He visited God's Holy Place. As he says himself, things did not change "till" he took that step. This is the Asaph Moment. That "till" sounds like it may have been a while in coming. Maybe it's the same for you? When were you last in God's Holy Place?

You no longer have to run to the Temple and sacrifice a sheep – you are God's temple: "All of you surely know that you are God's temple and that his Spirit lives in you" (1 Corinthians 3:16, CEV).

The easiest thing to do is to look inside yourself and have a meeting with the Christ in you, as Paul talks about in Galatians 2:20. Sometimes it can be helpful to have a special meeting place, a place without distractions, that will help you enter into God's presence. You may find a ritual helps you, like regularly reciting a prayer written in advance. It is important that you have these Asaph moments every so often so that you actually enter the Holy Place and open yourself to God.

How do you experience Christ in you? When did you meet with him last? Where did that meeting take place?

The Holy Place inside you is, ultimately, nothing more than a meeting place for you and Jesus, an encounter with the new you, whom I described in detail in my previous book, *Unfinished*.

Try to find out where and how to access this place within you where you can meet with God. He is really waiting to meet you. He says so in his Word: "Loving Me empowers you to obey my word. And my Father will love you so deeply that we will come to you and make you our dwelling place" (John 14:23, TPT).

When did you last visit God within you? How could you intentionally include these visits in your daily routine?

THE HOLY PLACE INSIDE YOU

It all boils down to us remembering and immersing ourselves in God's presence so that we learn to hear God's voice. This is what Christian mystics discovered and have written about through the centuries. They called this *oratio mentalis* – "mental prayer". This means focusing your inner self completely on God. The Orthodox church still widely uses the so-called Jesus Prayer, in which you practise internal prayer. As you inhale, you silently speak, "Lord Jesus Christ," and when you exhale, you say, "Have mercy." The goal is for this prayer to become automatic as you breathe so that the challenge from 1 Thessalonians 5:17 (NIV) to "pray continually" becomes your reality as the soul continues to pray subconsciously. While some of my friends have had good experiences with this kind of prayer, I always stumble when I try to sync the individual words with my heartbeat. I am simply not good enough at multitasking to do that. When I have tried, I almost forget to keep breathing, and that is not ideal in the long term.

It is not my intention to give you a list of concrete options for "mental prayer" – I encourage you to go on your own journey of discovery. Still, the most fascinating aspect for me has been finding this "inner space", the place where God lives in me. That is where I can meet with God, where I light that imaginary candle and spend time with him.

Dutch pastor and psychologist Henri Nouwen describes the posture of listening aptly:

> If we succeed at hearing and listening at least for a
> few minutes every day – right where we are now –
> we would discover that we are not alone and that
> the One who is with us wants only one thing: to give
> us love. Listening to the voice of love requires us to
> direct our hearts and minds to that voice.[13]

He suggests that we introduce a simple prayer into our day, like putting a burning candle in a dark room. It is our responsibility to make sure that, regardless of distractions, it doesn't go out.

Today we are constantly bombarded by stimuli, like hail beating down during a violent summer storm. This makes finding our inner Holy Place even more important, because it is a place of safety where we can retreat to recover and recuperate. Elizabeth of Dijon wrote:

> Like me, you have to build a small room inside of your soul. You then think that the dear God is present in it, and you enter it from time to time. If you feel your nerves or feel unhappy, then you flee quickly and entrust everything to the Master. Oh, if you had only a little knowledge of the right way to pray, then you would not find it boring. To me, it feels like resting, relaxing. You merely go to the one you love. One stays close to him, like a child in the arms of his mother, and then lets his heart run wild.[14]

Have you discovered this inner place for yourself yet? It has become one of my most important forms of prayer – going into stand-by mode in the middle of my daily routine and diving into myself for a few moments. I don't need a special place – although that can certainly be helpful – or special surroundings. I just take a seat in that inner place and light that candle. It doesn't take hours, sometimes not even minutes. And sometimes I don't manage to take even those few moments to myself. My thoughts fly around wildly without stopping. Then I find a way to concentrate on that candle again, a way to fight the persistent darkness, and I find myself surrounded again by a brightly shining peace. My prayer is often just a simple "Jesus".

Nouwen also writes that we can learn to recognize "that there is a place in us where God lives and where we are invited to live with him. One day we will come to see this inner, holy place as the most beautiful and dearest place we can go to spend time and be strengthened spiritually."

Maybe this is all a bit too mystical for you. Still, I want to encourage you to take the first step on the inward journey – to God and to yourself.

I like the words of the Carmelite nun and mystic Saint Teresa of Ávila, who wrote the following in the sixteenth century: "Had I known earlier, what I now know, that the tiny palace of my soul harboured such a great king, then I would not have left him alone so often." Imagine what this room looks like. What do you see around you on the way there? What do you see when you stand at the entrance to the room? When you arrive there, take a moment to light a candle and just enjoy. Pray, but most of all, listen.

Remember, it is about getting to know God better, learning to love him more. If you want to get to know someone better, you cannot just collect information about that person. The best way is to spend time together. When you spend time with God, it will automatically expand your image of him and will always take you into his surprising New Land.

Where does your image of God need an update?
Where and how do you meet with him personally?

It is worthwhile to stop by regularly and have a look at your inner room. "God is always in us, but we are so rarely at home."[15] Meeting God in your inner place means that he will take you on a voyage of discovery – not only to himself, but also to yourself, to your heart. We will talk about that more in the next chapter.

5

CARDIOGENIC

The Heart Territory

NEWLANDIC

You probably don't realize it, but you are constantly experiencing renewal. If you are an average person, you have about 100,000 hairs on your head. Each of these grows about 1 mm every three days. That means every day you have 30 m of new hair on you head, or 1 km in a month.[16] OK, maybe you belong to a species for whom there have been no dramatic advances in the area of hair growth for a while; then we can always look at the skin. In the time it takes to read this sentence, over 50,000 skin cells have been renewed. You lose 14 g of dead skin every day. That is millions of cells! After about one month, you have an entirely new set of cells on the surface of your skin. When you reach eighty, you will have lost about 400 kg of skin. That is not such a bad thing if you consider what would happen if we never lost any of those cells but they still kept reproducing all the time. You would probably make a good sumo wrestler in that case.

Our skin and hair clearly demonstrate how important renewal is for us. What our bodies do outwardly needs to happen inwardly as well. This has to do with our new spirit and the new heart that we receive from God (Ezekiel 36:26). Just like a computer, you need to download regular heavenly updates to renew your programming, to stay virus-free, and to be able to keep growing. Paul expresses it in this way: "For even though our outer person gradually wears out, our inner being is renewed every single day" (2 Corinthians 4:16, TPT).

This is a fascinating verse with a groundbreaking message. Our inner self is programmed for daily renewal—just like our skin and hair! Allowing this to happen, even actively participating in the process, is the best thing we can do. Unfortunately, we do not always take this inner renewal seriously, although this approach is completely normal in other aspects of our lives.

I haven't met many people who say, "Nah, I'm not going to change my underpants today. I always do that on the first of the month." God made renewal to be a natural part of your inner self, too. It is an ongoing process of reformation for both your spirit and your heart. It is in no way strenuous. Breathing, your heart beating, and eating are also natural, repetitive processes, and they are all life-giving and helpful, even pleasant.

Last summer, I was in Iceland standing on the continental rift, the point where the Eurasian and American plates meet. Actually, it is not quite accurate to say they meet there since the two land masses drift apart by about 2 cm annually. Over time, a large rift, many kilometres long, has developed and filled with lava – New Land in its truest form. Standing there, I suddenly understood that God wants to do something similar with my inner self. He stretches our hearts and spirits, widening them in all directions; he also moves our border markers, if we allow him to. And as the continental plates of our hearts slowly drift apart, often unnoticed, new space is formed – New Land Heart Territory. We need to intentionally enter into this new territory, occupy it, and put down roots. It will be empty, and perhaps even desolate, at first, but God brings clarity and life into that space just as he did at Creation. Although there was only formless, empty chaos at first, things changed when God spoke. He separated light from darkness and introduced coherent definition.

In order to make your New Land fruitful, you also need to allow God to speak his life-bringing words into your life, then accept them and give them room to grow.

THE JOURNEY OF THE HEART

The inward journey is an essential part of the faith life and is necessary for survival. If we do not pay attention to our inner self, allowing God to constantly renew us, then things begin to die away. Our lives become powerless, indeed lifeless. "Pay attention to the welfare of your innermost being, for from there flows the wellspring of life" (Proverbs 4:23, TPT). Our inner self is the starting point for everything we do outwardly. If we are "clean" inside, then our lives bring much fruit and we spread life around us. When God replaced Saul with a new king, he didn't look at outward characteristics, but he searched for a person whose heart yearned for God. "People judge others by what they look like, but I judge people by what is in their hearts" (1 Samuel 16:7, CEV). Life automatically flows from this kind of heart. This is also what God sees when he looks at you. That is why you should pay more attention to your heart than to anything else: invest at least as much time with God looking into your heart as you spend looking in the mirror to fix your outward appearance. Your heart is the source of all your actions and words.

Lots of people are obsessed with their performance – either consciously or unconsciously. How do I come across to others? What do people think about what I do? What do they think of me? Where do I need to do better in order to be more popular, or for God to love me more? Does anyone see what I am doing for God? Does God even see it? But God asks you the same question over and over again: where is your heart? Or, as Jesus posed the question to Peter, "Simon son of John, do you love me?" (John 21:15–17, CEV)

What's going on in your heart?

How do you answer Jesus' question, "Do you love me?"

Your heart is like a garden – only the good that has been sown there grows there. If you want to see good fruit grow, then you need to sow good seed or plant good seedlings. You cannot dig a hole and throw in a couple of rotten potatoes and expect lovely red tomatoes to grow. You also have to tend to what you have planted, feed, and water it, otherwise, it will not flourish, or other plants and weeds will take over. That's probably not what you want. I have learned this lesson in my own garden and in other areas of my personal life. Just because I eat a croissant every morning, it doesn't mean that I will be able to speak fluent French the next time I go to France. I have to invest time learning French words on my language app. The same goes for my body. I want to stay fit and healthy, but to do that, I need to exercise. If I only eat croissants and don't exercise, then both my French and my physical shape will probably deteriorate.

You have to invest in the right things in order to go through life with a healthy heart. Seeking God's heart is key in this process. We need to fill our hearts with his thoughts and promises so that they take root in our lives, grow, and bear fruit.

Anyone who sets off on a New Land journey will inevitably also visit his or her own heart along the way. This journey takes us to God and to ourselves. We will only go as far as we have already come to know him and ourselves. The length of our journey depends on the extent to which we are secure in our identity in him. This determines how much we will be able to walk in the things he has prepared for us. It's like a tree – it can only grow tall with branches that reach up to the sky if, at the same time, the roots are going deeper and deeper in the opposite direction.

This makes this verse in Jeremiah 4:3 even more interesting – "Break up your unploughed ground and do not sow among thorns" – and the verses that follow contain an exciting challenge: "Circumcise yourselves to the Lord, circumcise your hearts" (Jeremiah 4:4, NIV). God compares New Land to our hearts. For many years I was secretly convinced that my understanding of God and of faith was greater than the Christians around me. I thought that it was important to be very clear in certain topics and to communicate that clear position; I wanted to protect the truth of the faith. Naturally, there are core convictions of faith that should be preserved, but I discovered false motives behind a lot of my dearly held views. It turned out to be a hidden lack of love for others, an inner insecurity, and a sense of arrogance.

In all the years I have been walking with God, he has continually led me to these areas and gently asked whether I am ready to have that part of my heart circumcised. Thank God that he is so wonderfully patient and loving toward me. It is immensely important that we show others the same kind of patience and love as we walk with them on the journey of faith. We shouldn't always expect that they will go through the same processes and steps as we did. Instead, we should learn to trust that God dwells in other people and is at work – we are not the ones who do the work, who live in them, or who have to endure slow changes. He does it. He loves doing it. He is good at it. And he is far more patient, merciful, and loving than we are.

God is concerned about your New Land – what is going on inside you. The outward circumcision that was commanded in the Old Testament was worthless if not accompanied by an inward circumcision of the heart (Romans 2:29). Jesus sharply criticized religious behaviour that was separate from a living faith or a correct attitude of the heart. Being right in a religious sense is useless as long as the inner self is not right with God.

Rituals can be helpful for our faith, but they need to grow out of the right kind of soil. The crux of the matter is the heart. This is why Paul prays for the Ephesians' inner power and strength: "I pray that his Spirit will make you become strong followers and that Christ will live in your hearts because of your faith. Stand firm and be deeply rooted in his love" (Ephesians 3:16b–17, CEV). God is at work in us with his inexhaustible power, and he can do so much more than we could ever ask for or imagine, as Paul goes on to describe in verse 20. It is much more impressive to invite God into our areas of weakness and give him free rein than to try desperately to be a nicer, more religious person. Of course, it is also not right to let ourselves become lazy or passive and expect God to produce the change. But if he does not actively work on and in us through his Spirit, then we will only ever see minimal change in many areas.

Without the inward journey, the outward journey remains unfruitful. The journey to your heart is also the key to the journey to your true identity, who you really are before God, and what he intends to do with you and through you. So many Christians have not even begun to discover their full potential.

GOD'S VIEW

Imagine you order a pizza to be delivered, and it arrives without a box, hanging limply over the arm of the delivery driver, all the toppings falling onto the ground; the only tomato sauce you can see is running down their shirt. Never underestimate the value of a pizza box. Its value is defined by its identity, and its identity has to do with where it comes from and what's inside. It is the same with you. Your identity is defined by where you come from and by what you have inside. You come from God in that you are born of God (John 1:14), and Christ is inside you (John 1:13). These two things define how unbelievably valuable you are.

Jesus always went to people to give them a broader understanding of their identity. He meets Peter and immediately tells him who he is: "Simon son of John, you will be called Cephas" (John 1:42, CEV). *Cephas* is the Hebrew word for Peter and means "rock". God intended Peter to be a rock and wanted to build the church on him. For Peter, who often missed the mark in his overzealousness, that was certainly Terra Incognita, unknown New Land, but God knew exactly what he had put inside Peter.

One of my favourite "let me tell you about your true identity" stories in the Bible is about Gideon (Judges 6:11ff, NIV). While he was threshing wheat, an angel appeared to him and greeted him with the following words: "The Lord is with you, mighty warrior!" What a greeting! Especially since Gideon was anything but a warrior – mighty or not. All of Israel was hiding from the Midianites in the mountains in caves, canyons, and forts. Up to that point, Gideon had not shown himself as a great liberator of his people like Samson, who cleared Israel's enemies out of the way time and time again. Instead, Gideon kept a low profile like the rest of his countrymen and threshed his wheat in secret.

Maybe that angelic greeting sounded a bit sarcastic to him, or at least ironic. In any case, he did not react to it but started whining about his situation and questioning God's wisdom. The angel replied that Gideon possessed the strength needed to change the situation and that God had sent him to do so (verse 14).

But Gideon didn't jump on the bandwagon immediately; instead he offered lots of reasons why he was not a hero – from coming from the smallest tribe to being the youngest in his family.

Whenever I read this passage, I have the feeling that Gideon just wanted to get rid of that angel standing in front of him. He just didn't believe what he was hearing. He asked God for a sign, and then offered to cook the angel a meal of tender, young goat. But preparing a young goat takes a while – more than an hour in the steamer. When we were in the Philippines, we spent a week out in the countryside. The people there prepared two young goats for a party. My kids had petted those goats, looked out for them every morning, and now they were on a platter in front of us. Now they know that meat doesn't just come from the supermarket. We watched as they drained the blood, as three men skinned the animals and put them in boiling water, how they chopped them into pieces with a small axe... I eventually had to leave with the two smallest girls when I noticed that they were getting a bit pale. The whole process took hours, and we didn't eat the meal until the next day. Gideon couldn't have done it much faster himself. I think he was trying to take as much time as possible so that the angel would just get fed up and disappear – along with the assignment from God. Unfortunately for Gideon, the goat strategy did not work, and he didn't just get one sign of confirmation, but many.

What would you have done in Gideon's position?
How would you have responded to God's encouraging

statement about your identity? Would it have been easy to accept? Or do you trust what people say about you more?

I have caught myself at times trying to wriggle out of situations and hiding from God. God spoke to Gideon twice about his identity – about things that were not yet visible to other people or to Gideon himself. But God had planted the warrior identity in Gideon long ago, before anyone else could see it.

I spent my youth in the YMCA. I was a co-leader when I heard that the main leader was leaving in a couple of months. Although I already had a good deal of experience as a leader both in my job and otherwise, I didn't see myself as a leader at all back then. Out of fear of being forced to take over the leadership role, I handed in my resignation and quit the YMCA before the leader left.

Our own thoughts and the voices of those around us – whether positive or negative – can lead us astray. God's voice, though, will always lead us to the truth about ourselves, directly to our Newlandic identity.

When Paul began sharing the gospel, he chose to listen to God's voice: "We didn't speak to please people, but to please God who knows our motives" (1 Thessalonians 2:4b, CEV).

What aspects of the Newlandic identity that God has put in you have you already discovered?

We often look longingly at other people's qualities, thinking they are somehow more attractive than what we have been given. God doesn't make mistakes, though. He has thought everything through carefully. Don't waste your energy trying to live someone else's life. Instead, discover the power of living in what God has already planted in you.

What would God say to you about your true identity?

SPILT MILK

"God's love has been poured out into our hearts through the Holy Spirit, who has been given to us," says Romans 5:5 (NIV). This translation is a bit inaccurate, though. The original does not say that God's love has been poured into our hearts from the outside, but, instead, poured out from within our hearts. Let me explain this nuance a bit more because it really makes a difference. The original Greek says *en tais kardiaís*, in our hearts, which is a description of the location, not of who or what receives the action. This means that the action – pouring out – comes from within.

The other evening at the dining table, my daughter was playing with her cup of hot chocolate. All of a sudden the contents of her cup were flowing across the table onto the living room floor. Looking at the situation from the outside, you could say that "My daughter's hot chocolate was poured into our home." But that's just a bit off, like the translation of the verse in Romans, which actually says, "My daughter's hot chocolate was poured out in our home."

The idea here is that nobody stood over our dining table holding a giant watering can filled with hot chocolate and poured this into our house. Instead, the hot chocolate was already there, in a cup on the table, and that is where it was spilt. It is the same with God's love and your identity. It doesn't get poured in from the outside by some kind of heavenly pitcher. No, it is already inside you through God's Spirit, an inexhaustible wellspring that began flowing when you received Christ into your heart. That is where it gets poured out. And this fact makes a big difference for your identity. You need to realize that it comes from the inside out. You can learn to trust it and live out of it.

Let God pour out this love inside you. More and more, without stopping. This will give you an indestructible foundation, a fundamental identity that is clear and basic. "God's Spirit doesn't make us servants who are afraid of him. Instead, we become his children and call him our Father" (Romans 8:15, CEV).

Everybody has a different role to fulfil in his or her life. I am a husband, father, friend, director of a missionary organization, preacher, tennis player, etc. All of these things are built on my primary identity as a child of God that was given to me. My purpose in life has been developed out of that. That is how Jesus did it, too. He didn't simply begin doing miracles, but started working in his power after he heard God's statement about his identity, "This is my own dear Son, and I am pleased with him" (Matthew 3:17, CEV). God confirmed Jesus' true identity, which enabled Jesus to live powerfully out of a clearly defined identity that was firmly anchored in the Father.

When I get home, four little girls with bright eyes usually come running toward me, shouting, "Papa, Papa!" and wrapping themselves around my legs. Those are wonderful moments for a father as you feel that your children really miss you and need you. God's Father-heart longs for us to run to him and throw our arms around him, too, as we cry out, "Abba, Daddy!"

I also try to encourage my daughters in their identity, just as God confirmed his Son's identity, by telling them that they are my beloved children. And as daughters of the King of Kings, they are also princesses. So I usually say, "Good night, Princess So-and-so" when I tuck them into bed.

And I know that they have got the message. In certain European countries at Epiphany, Christians commemorate the three wise men or kings who brought their gifts to the baby Jesus. They eat cake that has individual segments, and one has a small king figurine baked into it. Whoever gets the segment with the king is crowned "king for a day". When they celebrated Epiphany in my daughter's kindergarten in January, our neighbours' son remarked that they also had a cake at home. Without skipping a beat, my daughter answered, "We don't have one, but we're all princesses already anyway." She had taken her identity to heart.

Sometimes we haven't quite understood that last part – we are God's children, his princes and princesses – but we're not the king ourselves. This often brings confusion in life. We want to be the king or queen ourselves. We want to reign, to make the rules, and to decide how things should be. We want to be in charge of who gets to come into the kingdom and whose visa is denied.

Up to the point when Jesus heard "This is my dear Son…" he hadn't yet performed even the slightest miracle. There is no mention of Jesus parting the waters in his bath, changing his milk into orange juice at breakfast, or multiplying his chocolate bar a hundred-fold to share with the other schoolchildren. He lived like a regular person. But he still carried that identity as the "Son of the Heavenly Father" inside himself.

It's the same with my daughters; their position as my children does not depend on what they do. When my oldest came home with a drawing, I just blurted out, "Wow! What a fantastic house! That's great!" Since the second oldest also likes hearing that kind of reaction from me, she came running a few minutes later with something in hand. She had taken a couple of pieces of paper and glued them together, but it was impossible to figure out what it was supposed to be. Of course I didn't say, "Oh, yuck! What is this supposed to be?" My reaction had nothing to do with the result of her work, and I said exactly the same kinds of things I had told her older sister: "Wow! Look how well you glued this together! That's great!" I did not want to compare their achievements but to honour their efforts. Even more, I wanted to encourage and praise them because they are my daughters. It is not a matter of what you do or don't do. God loves you as his daughter or son. The question is why you don't always allow his love to reach your heart and shower you unconditionally. Search for this unending spring of love inside yourself so that your true identity becomes clear.

BEING A CHILD

The idea that the creator God offers each of us the opportunity to be adopted into his family is enormously powerful. And although many people have accepted this adoption offer, they do not always understand that they are also given a new identity, and that their new identity is a foundation to live on. They do not live as sons and daughters of the heavenly Father, but still as servants.

> *And because you are sons, God has sent forth into our hearts the Spirit of His Son, crying, 'Abba, Father!' [7] Therefore you are no longer a servant, but a son, and if a son, then an heir of God through Christ.*
> (Galatians 4:6–7, MEV)

Basically, a servant waits for three things – an order, a wage, and time off. We can see this pattern in the lives of many Christians, too. We wait for God to give us an order, and we don't dare to decide our own actions. Of course, it seems very pious to wait on God for an answer, but God has also given us a certain responsibility for our own lives as co-heirs with Jesus. My kids don't come to me every five minutes to ask what they should play with next. They are allowed to do what they want; what they enjoy. And, as their father, I am simply there to watch the circus taking place on the trampoline or the badminton match in the car park or even as they make a 2-metre-long paper plane.

Sometimes we feel like we deserve a wage from God, and we spend a lot of time waiting around for our work to pay off in some way. "I've been working in my church for twenty years, and now this has happened to me?" We think that God ought to be really happy that we follow him. We tally up all our services and activities to hold up in God's face whenever something unpleasant happens to us. "C'mon, God. You've got to be kidding! You can't do this to me. After all, I've…!" This is a prime example of servant thinking.

The third thing a servant expects is free time – just like those Christians who think they need time off from their faith or their strenuous church life. Maybe your time off is the time between church services, from Monday to Friday, or perhaps on holiday. You decide to take a "faith sabbatical" or a short break to do all the things you think are not appropriate for the Christian lifestyle.

Being a servant is unbelievably strenuous in the long term. God did not call us to be his servants, but to be his children. We shouldn't wait around for an order or for our wages since we are already co-heirs of everything he has. And we certainly shouldn't need time off from being a child of God. Take a look at the example of the two brothers in Luke 15 (CEV), who obviously did not understand what it meant to be sons of the father.

The first wants his wages, or his share of the inheritance. This is clearly servant language. He wants to get away, to have some time off and create some distance between him and the father. He is looking for New Land and adventure, but he doesn't see that he already lives in New Land and that the real adventure would be in investigating what is all around him.

Then he hits rock bottom and wonders whether he can even dare to go home to his father. He thinks that he can only go back as a servant, no longer as a son. This reveals that he really doesn't know his father, even though he was brought up by him. If he really knew him, he would know that his dad misses him terribly.

The son practises his speech, "Father, I have sinned against God in heaven and against you," and heads home. But, before he gets a chance to speak, he is in his father's arms. "But when he was still a long way off, his father saw him and felt sorry for him. He ran to his son and hugged and kissed him" (Luke 15:20, CEV). Finally, he mumbles his sentence, which he had probably repeated the whole way home as he ran through his father's different possible reactions in his head, but I bet it was hard to hear him when he said it, since his face was buried in his father's chest. In any case, the father wants nothing to do with the ridiculous offer, and he calls him "my son". That's answer enough.

What about you – do you know the Father? Are you aware of your identity as a daughter or son?

The heavenly Father misses you terribly when you go out to run around on your own and end up back in those old patterns of slavery. Do you truly believe that he will always forgive you and receive you back with tears in his eyes?

The second son had the same problem – he whines over the fact that his brother gets a whole host of gifts when he returns home. He doesn't understand that everything already belongs to him. He acts like a servant who has completed his tasks for the father very diligently but is ultimately unhappy with the wages he receives. "Look, these many years I have served you, and I never disobeyed your command" (Luke 15:29, ESV).

I find the father's reaction to the son's emotional eruption and servant language very moving: "My son, you are always with me, and everything I have is yours" (verse 31). This "My son" is the direct answer to his servant-like approach. He speaks to both young men as his sons, confirming their identity.

We often underestimate our position as sons and daughters and fail to fully understand the added dimension and power our identity brings to our lives. Lots of problems in life stem from the fact that we have not clarified our identity or perhaps because we have only agreed to the adoption into God's family on paper, without ever changing from servant mode to a real son or daughter.

I asked my six-year-old once, "Do you know that I love you to the moon and back?" To which she replied, a bit annoyed, "Sure, Papa! You tell me that every day!" That is exactly what I try to do, because the feeling of being loved by a parent can give you great stability and security in life, which leads to a healthy identity. How much more should this be true of knowing you are loved as a child of the heavenly Father? We need to know our Father's heart.

What are you living as – a child of the heavenly Father or as a servant?

In which areas are you acting like a servant? In which areas are you not yet enjoying freedom?

In Exodus 13:3, God tells his people to always commemorate that day when he led them out of slavery in Egypt. This event is a picture of what God wants to do in your life, too. He wants to lead each of us out of slavery and into freedom. This makes our running toward different dependencies even more counterproductive than we think. The Israelites also wanted to return to slavery; the more they remembered it, the better it seemed. In the end, it even seemed better than depending on God, their provider. The only true freedom we can find is dependence upon God.

In the Bible, the word "slave" is often synonymous with the word "servant". Paul, Peter, and John sometimes described themselves as God's slaves. Being God's slave is a good thing, because it reflects a readiness to serve him. However, it does not mean that we should fall into servant-thinking with regard to our identity.

We have not received a narrowing spirit that takes away all our freedom, but instead a spirit that makes us sons and daughters of God. Paul writes in 1 Corinthians 7:23 (TPT), "Since a great price was paid for your redemption, stop having the mind-set of a slave." Today many people enslave themselves through obsessive behaviours, addictions, unhealthy dependencies, or by living according to the opinions of other people, getting caught up in worrying what other people think or allowing others to determine what they do. Does this sound familiar? Are there people in your life whom you respect to an almost unhealthy extent because you act differently when they are around? You can't be yourself anymore and you speak and act a little differently. You have become enslaved. The pressure to please people, the fear of people's opinions and their power over you, is one of the greatest epidemics in our world – these things spring from a lack of understanding and immersion in God's love and in the identity God offers as a daughter or son.

God wants to lead us out of this kind of slavery into freedom. You are a child who does not have to impress the Father or anyone else because you know that you are 100 per cent loved. This is your true identity.

Understanding the full scope and power of our identity as a daughter or son of God is the ultimate goal as we discover more and more of the Heart Territory. Have you learned to say, "Abba, dear Father!" and really mean it?

FAITH IN GOD

A friend of mine is a photographer and often takes pictures of celebrities. He regularly photographs the Basel football team and has got to know them pretty well. He once took his son Ruben along on a photo shoot, where they met Marco Streller, one of the most well-known players in Swiss football at the time. Marco, who had already heard about Ruben from my friend, went up to the boy and said, "Hi, you must be

Ruben!" To which the boy responded, "Yeah, but who are you?" An unclear identity can lead to confusion in life.

If your foundational identity as a child of God is not clear, then you will never be able to enter New Land. Once, when I was speaking at a big event, the doorman wasn't going to let me into the backstage area because I had forgotten my wristband. The problem was, though, that I was the main speaker and needed to be on stage in a couple of minutes. Identity is so important! Far too often we go through life without being aware of our identity in God. It is not just about believing in him as the one who shapes you and gives you an identity, but it is much more about realizing that God believes in you.

In 1965, American psychologists Robert Rosenthal and Lenore Jacobson studied the impact that teachers have on their students and vice versa.[17] In one primary school, teachers were told that, based on testing, it was clear that about 20 per cent of their students were about to have a developmental breakthrough. These so-called "bloomers" could be expected to make great advances in the coming school year. However, the students had just been selected at random. But after one year, those students had made significant improvements; 47 per cent of the "bloomers" increased their IQ score by twenty or more points, and some 21 per cent even raised their scores by thirty points or more. As a whole, the achievements of these students were significantly greater than the rest of the class. There was only one possible explanation for this improvement: the teachers' expectations of those particular students, which impacted the way they dealt with them. This experiment has come to be known as the "Pygmalion effect".

God believes in you. Just like with the Pygmalion effect, if we trust his faith in us, then we have more confidence to perform better in life.

I experience this again and again when people around me working on projects or in leadership roles rise to the occasion, leaving behind mediocrity to do great things, just because they were surrounded by people who believed in them. This is why we try to create a culture at Campus für Christus Switzerland that motivates our staff to try new things and to look for the God-given potential inside them, even if it is still hidden. When people feel that someone believes in them, they are empowered to perform at levels that sometimes surprise even them.

It is important which people you allow to speak into your life about your identity, because those statements can have a profound impact on you – either positive or negative. It all depends on whom you believe. People tend to accept vague and general statements as an accurate description of themselves (this is the reason for the popularity of all those horoscopes in magazines and newspapers). Each of us is the target of opinions and ideas from different people every day. We read and hear things about ourselves, sense unspoken expectations, take note of requirements, make guesses about what others think of our behaviour, and, in reality, we are always in danger of accepting these things as fact. It is immensely important to understand that it is not only **what** we believe that matters, but also **whom** we believe. The direction you point your inner self toward will determine what shapes and influences your life and your identity. It is vital that you expose yourself to the thoughts God has about you. They are true because he sees your innermost self. And when he speaks to you, he does not see the sinner and the failure; instead, he sees the true identity he planted in you. As your loving Father, God overlooks all the dirt and stink of the pigsty, and he takes you lovingly in his arms, showing you your worth and giving you the assurance that you are his child.

He is the one who gives us our identity. Your life will receive unimaginable power when you live out of this identity as a daughter or son of God. This identity unfolds in your life because God believes in you, and, as you begin to trust the faith he has in you, you will also expose yourself to the thoughts he has about you.

People at events always tell me that they have never felt worthy of being God's son or daughter. Just like the Prodigal Son, they think they cannot have access to God as their Father because of their life history, their personality, or their behaviour. If you also think this is true, then you have misunderstood the mercy of our heavenly Father and the power of forgiveness at the cross. God's grace is infinitely greater than our sin. The dimensions of his forgiveness exponentially exceed the size of our failure. The question is not whether or not he will forgive you, but why you refuse to allow yourself to be forgiven.

If you immerse yourself in this grace, you will not only find God but also yourself – you will find the way into your own true identity.

When you lie down and go to sleep at night or when you wake up each morning, do you believe that God has faith in you? In these special moments of stillness, do you immerse yourself in his peace?

What is stopping you from immersing yourself in that peace and in your God-given identity right now? Trust God. He believes in you.

THE IDENTITY TRIP

The inward journey is often underestimated. Many people constantly ask themselves where they want to go. But the most important question is not "Where am I going?"; rather, it is "Who am I?" The "Who" always precedes the "Where", because the "Who" determines your "What". This applies to people as well as organizations. Inspirational author Richard Rohr said, "When you get your 'Who am I?' question right, all of your 'What should I do?' questions tend to take care of themselves." For as long as we do not know our true identity, we will continue to do things in our lives that do not yield much fruit.

At the Forest Animal Olympics, a little rabbit performs badly in the swimming competition and comes in last place in the tree-climbing event. He will only be successful when he recognizes his identity as a rabbit and starts competing in events like hopping or breeding! What you do with your life and whether or not you are successful depends wholly on who you are. Our "What" is determined by the "Who", or possibly by our own idea of the "Who". That is why it is so important to find out exactly what the "Who" really is.

Perhaps you often ask yourself, "What should I do?" or "What can I do well?" But the question that will automatically lead you in the right direction is neither What nor Where, nor even good old Why; rather, the only question that will help is Who! Who I am, and who he is in me. When you begin to discover who made you and what he intended you to be, then why you were made becomes clear, too.

Finding and living out your calling depends on you finding your own identity first. That word "calling" tends to make me a bit nervous, actually. Young people in particular often end up searching for their one and only special calling without ever realizing that people in the Bible are sometimes not very happy about the calling they receive. Moses, for example, fought against his, and Jonah tried to run away.

The term "calling" can sometimes lead us down the wrong path, especially if you connect your calling with a long-term sense of joy and fulfilment. And if you don't find that, then it is possible to go through life and completely miss your intended purpose. Many people end up being paralysed and don't know what to do with their lives because they are so focused on waiting for that one specific thing. However, life is what happens while you are waiting on your calling to reveal itself. And, instead of a big, enlightening calling announcement, some people just need a jump start to get things moving.

It's not really about a great calling or the question of whether you are in the right place or not, but whether you are living out of your identity and allowing your charisma to run free right where you are. The biggest challenge is that many do not really know what their God-given charisma is: the difference their true identity can make. Charisma comes from the Greek word *chárisma* and means a gift of grace from God. Something special given by God. You could ask yourself, "What makes me feel alive?" "What things do not sap my energy but give me more power?" and "What brings life to people around me when I do it?"

When you have found these answers, you are well on your way to identifying your own charisma.

Trying to conform to a specific image is inherently stressful, but even being yourself takes quite a bit of energy. There are newspaper reports from 1918 that tell an unconfirmed story of how Charlie Chaplin entered himself into a Charlie Chaplin look-alike contest at a regional carnival somewhere in the US.[18] The main event of the competition was imitating the unique Chaplin walk. I watched all those jerky, old-fashioned films when I was a kid, and, afterwards, I often tried to copy that walk in my living room, armed with an umbrella.

In the competition, Chaplin was surprisingly unable to convince the judges with his imitation of himself. He finished in twentieth place! Even I probably would have beaten him with my childish imitation. But that is exactly the problem: whenever we try to "play" ourselves, the act requires effort and is doomed to fail. The only way things run smoothly is when we stop trying to play a desired character and just allow Christ in us to live. This is what brings life to us and to those around us. Everything flows out of Christ into our inner selves.

Having a clear idea of our identity results in a life that runs smoothly, without friction. So much of what makes us afraid of living our own identity has to do with feelings of shame. This is the reason why we hide, and it keeps us from feeling like we belong. Shame can also be abused by leaders of organizations or churches in an effort to wield power. People paralysed by shame do not suffer because of what they do (that is actually guilt), but because of who they are. Shame leads us to dead ends and fears that hinder us from living in redeemed relationships. When we talk about the New Land No-Fear Zone, then we have to talk about a Shame-

Free Zone as well. Finding our true identity gives us deep roots that help us open up to one another and allow us to be vulnerable with one another. The best antidote to a shame-filled culture is a clear identity in Christ. People who understand that they are God's beloved sons and daughters are no longer dogged by shame over their unfinished, imperfect selves. Dignity beats shame every time.

Do not allow yourself to suffocate under a thick, heavy blanket of shame in your life. Sort out your true identity with Jesus.

SCRAP METAL

Once you have conquered the Heart Territory, one of the most powerful negative factors in your life, fear of people, will lose its power over you. This topic comes up a few times in this book, and that's on purpose. I meet so many people who are driven by this particular fear. Fear of people cements the feet of your identity, stopping them in their tracks. I have intentionally made the decision to put off all forms of an enslaved spirit and fear of people and to submit myself only to the fear of God. Just as David writes in Psalm 86:11 (NIV), "Teach me your way, Lord, that I may rely on your faithfulness; give me an undivided heart, that I may fear your name." I want my heart to be undivided toward God, just like David's was, so that I fear his name. In the Gospels we find certain leaders who were afraid of confessing Jesus because they knew they would be banned from the synagogue. "Even then, many of the leaders put their faith in Jesus, but they did not tell anyone about it. The Pharisees had already given orders for the people not to have anything to do with anyone who had faith in Jesus. And besides, the leaders liked praise from others more than they liked praise from God" (John 12:42–43, CEV).

Jesus himself was impressively free of the fear of people. After his baptism and time in the desert, he returned to his hometown of Nazareth. That must have been a special moment. People had already started whispering about him, "Isn't he Joseph's son?" (Luke 4:22, CEV). Jesus entered the synagogue and, "coincidentally", he was given the scroll containing the writing of Isaiah to read from. That was an emotionally charged moment, because the men present had certainly heard all the stories about what Jesus had done. They could not reconcile those things with the young Jesus they had seen playing in the sand with his camel-shaped moulds. I think they were all curious and expectant about what he might say.

Jesus took the scroll, unrolled it, and began reading Isaiah 61:1–2 (see also Luke 4:18–19):

> *The Spirit of the Lord God has taken control of me! The Lord has chosen and sent me to tell the oppressed the good news, to heal the broken-hearted, and to announce freedom for prisoners and captives. This is the year when the Lord God will show kindness to us and punish our enemies.*
> (CEV)

Then he rolled up the scroll and sat down. That was one of those perfectly orchestrated, you-could-hear-a-pin-drop moments you see in Hollywood blockbusters. All eyes were fixed on Jesus. Maybe a couple of men even forgot to breathe for fear of missing what he said next. If he had waited too long, a couple of blue-in-the-face Scribes might have fallen off their stools. But all he said was, "What you have just heard me read has come true today."

Bam! A wave of euphoria broke out. Everyone started talking at once. They were impressed and amazed as they felt that his words were from God. Jesus could have easily savoured that euphoric moment.

If I had been in Jesus' place, I would certainly have locked eyes with Abner, my childhood rival who always pulled my hair and flattened my sandcastles, to see his nod of approval in my direction. But Jesus had an uncanny knack for ruining a good moment. He immediately announced that he would not be doing any of the signs and wonders in Nazareth that he had done elsewhere. (That is probably what some of the people had been hoping for.) He didn't want to put on a circus to satisfy the curiosity of a fickle crowd. Jesus did not do what would have pleased those people; rather, he followed the instructions he had received in order to please his Father. As a result, the initial amazement of the people quickly turned into anger, and they wanted to throw him off a nearby cliff.

Be and do what you are and not what others expect from you. Stop trying to make everyone happy. You are not a bar of chocolate. "Nothing makes us more cowardly and unconscionable than the desire to be loved by everyone," said Austrian author Marie von Ebner-Eschenbach.[19]

I have decided not to live for the applause of others but to strive to receive the enthusiastic and encouraging clapping of God's hands alone. Anyone who lives for the applause of others will suffocate in their criticism. Paul followed the same rule: "Am I now trying to win the approval of human beings, or of God? Or am I trying to please people? If I were still trying to please people, I would not be a servant of Christ." (Galatians 1:10, NIV)

The fear of people covers up your true identity; you can no longer see clearly, and you live only to please others. This is one of life's plan destroyers. The Bible confirms that clearly: "Fear of man will prove to be a snare, but whoever trusts in the Lord is kept safe" (Proverbs 29:25, NIV). We have to learn to swap our fear of people for a fear of God, because the fear of God is the only kind of fear that produces positive fruit in our lives.

I don't always manage it completely, but I realize that I have been able to take steps into New Land in this particular area. I am getting better at doing and saying what God puts on my heart, instead of just doing what I think people want to hear. The result is unbelievably liberating, like diving into my true identity, into what God has planted in me, and shaking off all those burdens that people have placed on me to make me into something or someone that I simply am not. "It is better to be hated for what you are than to be loved for what you are not," said French author André Gide.

When David volunteered to fight the giant Goliath, King Saul offered him his own royal suit of armour. When he put it on, David could hardly even walk, let alone fight. So he did the only thing he could; he turned to Saul:

> *'I can't move with all this stuff on,' David said. 'I'm just not used to it.' David took off the armour and picked up his shepherd's stick. He went out to a stream and picked up five smooth rocks and put them in his leather bag. Then with his sling in his hand, he went straight toward Goliath.*
> (1 Samuel 17:39–40, CEV)

His actions are impressive, even exemplary to me. Whenever people come and want to dress me up in something that doesn't really suit me, I need to be ready to take it off again and put on what fits me best. In David's case, it was his staff, his shepherd's bag, and his slingshot.

But often we are quite flattered when someone offers us a suit of armour. So many people jump into a new assignment or a particular role or take on a new project that God really didn't intend for them, something for which they have received neither the call nor the ability. But it feels good to say yes, because you are being offered the royal suit of armour.

Entering into Heart Territory does not mean putting on armour that doesn't fit you. Instead, it means discovering your true identity and then living to the fullest out of that place. It is fine if you fall back into that old slave/servant pattern now and again. Just allow yourself – your identity – to be renewed, especially in moments like that. Now, go and hang that oversized suit of armour back in the wardrobe. Or, better yet, just throw it out as scrap metal.

Off you go to explore your Heart Territory!

6 ROMANTIC

The Relationship Territory

The Relationship Territory is the most fiercely contested area of all, and not without reason. The real-life dramas that take place in relationships often have a spiritual component that we are not completely aware of. Now, I am not the type to look for demons lurking around every corner or interpret every dark cloud in the sky as a spiritual message, but even I can see the work of the Father of Lies, who takes every opportunity to turn our heads and sell us his false substitute for our relationships.

God wove together a fascinating fabric of relationships in his creation. He himself is very relational, as evidenced in the Trinity with God the Father, Jesus the Son, and the Holy Spirit, three in one. Then he created mankind as his counterpart in order to have a relationship with us. He even said from the beginning that it is not good for a person to be alone. That is why he put us into relationships. At the same time, every person has a relationship with him or herself. And we all have a relationship with the world around us and God's creation as a whole.

God created a world in which we live in relationship to God, to ourselves, to the people around us, and to his creation. He is a hopeless romantic. When sin came into the world, all four of these relationship levels were broken. The first people hid from God (relationship to God), they suddenly perceived themselves very differently, realizing they were naked (relationship to oneself), then they were driven out of Paradise (relationship to God's creation), and later, Cain killed his brother Abel (relationship to other people). These things all reflect the Devil's handiwork. He tries to convince us that we can do just fine without God and that we should stop listening to him when we make decisions. Unfortunately, this strategy is quite effective most of the time and causes us to commit the worst sin: to think we don't need God sends everybody on an "I-don't-need-God" trip, the true "mother of all sins", which leads to the breakdown of relationships. You can see this everywhere you look.

The Devil comes to destroy what God makes. He is not terribly creative, though. For example, God created sexuality as a wonderful thing for us, but the Devil's best idea is to simply pervert what God made. Unfortunately, even this clumsy and unimaginative scam is quite successful.

"The reason the Son of God was revealed was to undo and destroy the works of the devil" (1 John 3:8, TPT). As a former maths teacher, I like this equation. When Christ destroys what the Devil has destroyed, then we are already dealing with restoration since minus multiplied by minus gives us a plus.

Precisely because the relationship level is so contested, Jesus gives us the greatest commandment:

> **'Love the Lord your God with all your heart and with all your soul and with all your mind and with all your strength.' The second is this: 'Love your neighbour as yourself.' There is no commandment greater than these.**
> (Mark 12:30–31, NIV)

This is where the Devil brings out his massive attack force. He tries to torpedo Relationship Territory by pulling marriages and families apart. He tries to destroy the unity among Christians by turning us against one another. He sows seeds of envy, resentment, jealousy, thirst for power, dissatisfaction, hatred, greed, arrogance, pride, and lots of other negative things into our relationships. And, because we are generally inattentive and too lazy to pull out the weeds of our relationship gardens, we allow some of those seeds to germinate and take root.

The fact that the word Devil is used here is probably enough to upset some people. I am not interested in promoting a medieval image of personified Evil, but I do want to recognize the existence of evil as a twenty-first-century reality and not ignore it.

It is not a question of "moral sins" – what one may or may not do – but of this brokenness as a basic disease from which all humanity suffers. That is why God offers us reconciliation in Christ (2 Corinthians 5:18–19, NIV) and the wonderful gift of living in reconciled relationships.

Do you see any unhealthy plants growing in any of your relationships, something that doesn't belong, and which you need to weed out together with Jesus?

It is time to conquer the Relationship Territory and reclaim the land!

SEEING THROUGH GOD'S EYES

I often race through the day, focused on everything I have to get done, without really seeing those around me. As an experiment, Joshua Bell, an internationally famous violin virtuoso, disguised himself as a busker and played in a subway station in Washington like a common street musician. Most people did not recognize him and walked by without paying attention. Joshua, who regularly sells out huge concert venues, played for forty-three minutes to 1,097 passers-by and made $32 and some change.

That wouldn't even buy you one of the cheapest seats to one of his many symphonic concerts.

People just saw a nameless street musician and ignored him. In the same way, we often only allow a person to make a first impression and then never look any further to see the identity that God has planted in them. It works the same way for our own identity. We have to learn to see not only those around us, but also ourselves, through God's eyes, so that our relationships can function well. Often this requires us to learn a new way of thinking.

Paul had a clear idea of why he should travel to Macedonia. He had seen a man in a dream who asked him to come and help him (Acts 16). So he travelled there with Timothy to preach the gospel. They arrived in Philippi, a city with no synagogue. On the sabbath, they went down to a nearby river where they hoped to find people praying. I don't know exactly when Paul started to doubt whether he would meet that same man at all. When they got to the river, there was no sign of that man who had asked for help: instead, they just met a few women. One was called Lydia, a Greek who had converted to Judaism. God opened her heart, and she and her entire household accepted Paul's message and began to follow Jesus Christ.

Lydia is recognized as the first European believer in Jesus. She was a dealer in expensive purple cloth, and she was single, perhaps as a result of her job, as the production of purple cloth was a complicated process involving the extraction of the dye from a particular type of sea snail. The snails had to be caught alive so that the purple gland could be removed. Then it was crushed, cured in salt for three days and boiled for ten more days to extract the whitish substance to make the dye. The purple colour appeared during the drying process as it reacted with sunlight, but it also produced a disgusting smell that lingered for a long time. We can only imagine the odour Lydia must have given off! She wasn't just Lydia, but "Stinky Lydia".

There is a measurement for determining the intensity of odours called the "olf". One olf is the smell of a regular person based on a skin area of 1.8 m^2 and 0.7 baths per day. A smoker registers at 25 olf, and a sweaty athlete measures 30 olf. Lydia probably pushed the upper limit of the scale, maybe reaching 50 or 100 olf. She was probably working down by the river, where she met Paul, who was hoping to meet a few Jews there for their regular ritual cleansing. But this appointment was set up by God. First, both Paul and Lydia had to set aside their preconceived notions and look through God's eyes to see the Newlandic qualities in one another. Paul had travelled to a new continent, but he didn't meet the man he had expected, the one who needed help. And Stinky Lydia had to see herself through God's eyes; this woman, who was surrounded by horrible smells, probably didn't ever expect to become a "pleasing aroma" for Europe. She had to rethink everything about herself when she began to realize that God had seen her and was calling her to found his church on a new continent. Healthy relationships require Newlandic eyes.

Where have you allowed a dream to take you off track so that you are no longer able to see what God is up to?

Is there anyone you have put into a box based on a first impression? What relationships are you fed up with? What helps you to see yourself and others through God's eyes?

HOLDING UP THE TOWEL

In my marriage to Tamara there are romantic times and other times as well. Our different personalities often create conflict, but those differences are exactly why we got together. Sometimes I fall victim to the crazy idea that it would be good to be married to myself. The two of us would have such fun because we have the same sense of humour, the same talents, and the same likes and dislikes. I would only ever eat what I like, only watch the films I want to, and always say exactly what I want to hear. But that marriage would end tragically because we wouldn't be able to support each other in our areas of weakness. Instead, those negative qualities would be amplified like sound waves through a loudspeaker. Everything would quickly become one-sided and everyday life would be filled with tension. We need opposites in life. A cheerfully fitting example is the city partnership between a village in north-western Wales named Llanfairpwllgwyngyllgogerychwyrndrobwllllantysiliogogogoch (the longest place name in Europe) and the French village simply called Y. That Welsh tongue-twister was thought up by a shoemaker or tailor in the nineteenth century to promote tourism. It means "St Mary's Church in the hollow of the white hazel near the rapid whirlpool and the Church of St Tysilio of the red cave". And "Y" simply means… Y!

Learning to love our differences is one of the biggest secrets to a healthy relationship. It is not about adopting them yourself or approving blindly, but instead learning to embrace them because those differences are a reflection of God's multifaceted nature. When he as the holy God manages to love us in our imperfection, then we ought to at least try to do the same.

NEWLANDIC

At Campus für Christus Switzerland there were times when we stood in each other's ways; the organized people were annoyed by the chaotic side of the creative ones and the creative people felt hemmed in by what they saw as unnecessary structures. A system can escalate within itself so that, in the end, the desired cooperation becomes nothing more than an exercise in unhappiness for everyone involved. But then we experienced the powerful working of God's Spirit among us. Not only did some outward things happen, but the inward attitude of our hearts was changed so that we could see things from a new and better perspective. We no longer only saw the annoying imperfections in one another, but suddenly each individual's special strengths and unique contribution to the whole became visible. We began to build up a Newlandic culture in which people spoke openly about their limitations and allowed others to step into that space and fill the vacuum with their strengths and talents. The result has been a developing culture of cooperation, working with one another and being there for one another, leading to successful relationships that bear fruit. An internal workplace philosophy developed that we should protect one another by "holding up the towel" to cover someone's nakedness in their area of weakness or limitation.

In my book *Unfinished*, I wrote about the abyss of our weakness, which I described as our "inner pit bull". Similarly, we can see the new things that God gives us, our strengths, which I described as a "soaring eagle". When you live in fruitful, life-giving relationships, then you will become acquainted with the other person's pit bull, but you will also learn to see the eagle inside them that is ready to soar. It works the same with our inner selves, too.

**Scan through your current relationships and pick out one
that is having problems. In one column, make a list of all
the pit bulls you can see in the other person.
Then, in a second column, write down that person's
eagle qualities. If you can't identify any at all, then
ask God to show you some the next time you see that
person. How can you learn to see their eagle qualities
more clearly and to appreciate what that person has
to offer? How can you actively support that person by
"holding up the towel" to cover their weaknesses and
balance out their shortcomings?**

SPEAKING THE SAME LANGUAGE

Healthy relationships need to develop a common language.
If we can't understand the language of our partner, it is easy
to get tripped up and miss the intended destination. Jaeyaena
Beurageng from southern Thailand experienced this principle
very literally and painfully back in 1982 when she took the
wrong bus by mistake. Instead of going home, she ended up
1,200 km to the north in a place with the mellifluous name:
Krung Thep Mahanakhon Amon Rattanakosin Mahinthara
Ayuthaya Mahadilok Phop Noppharat Ratchathani Burirom
Udomratchaniwet Mahasathan Amon Piman Awatan Sathit
Sakkathattiya Witsanukam Prasit, better known as Bangkok
(there's another one for your list of unusually long place names).
When she arrived there, she managed to get on another wrong
bus and continued some 700 km further north to Chiang Mai.
Because she only spoke her southern Yawi dialect and didn't
understand a word of Thai, she was completely unable to

communicate with the people around her. After a five-year odyssey, she ended up homeless, living on the streets. Her husband and seven children had given her up for dead, until Jaeyaena met some students from her province who understood her and were able to inform her family. Her village prepared a joyful reception for her homecoming.

When two people do not speak the same language – either verbally or non-verbally – then a relationship immediately becomes very difficult. Sometimes Tamara and I find ourselves in the middle of a conflict that isn't really about a specific topic, but has more to do with the way we are communicating about that topic. People who are interested in working for Campus für Christus Switzerland and come to get a taste of how we do things are often shocked at our unusually direct way of communicating with one another. It is often the case that a "loving, Christian way of communicating" turns out to be beating around the bush, not addressing the difficult issues at hand. But this is completely wrong, since love's godly power only becomes visible when paired with truth and clarity. Of course, when you speak directly and clearly but the other person does not see that you are really on their side, then it is easy for people to feel offended.

My favourite communications disaster to date with Campus für Christus is legendary in its level of embarrassment... We had drafted a letter to all our ministry partners, both in German and in French. Unfortunately, the French translation was a bit too literal, and the greeting "Dear Supporters" in German ended up as "Dear Pimps" in French – yes, a kind of supporter, but certainly not what we wanted to communicate. So, our very important letter sent out to numerous addresses began with the greeting "Dear Pimps", definitely not the best way to ask people for donations and prayer.

It is so easy to underestimate the dynamics of communication. The sender and the recipient never hear exactly the same message because no one has a completely neutral ear. We all hear on multiple levels, formed by our own history and personality. According to Friedemann Schulz von Thun, a psychologist and communications expert, every message has four levels: factual, relationship, self-disclosure, and appeal. Asking Tamara the seemingly harmless and unsuspecting question "Did you do something different with your hair today?" could easily end in a drama of epic proportions, which both surprises and completely overwhelms me as a man. It's a matter of the level on which and with which ear Tamara hears my question.

Factual: She hears a completely objective enquiry whether she did something different with her hair and gives a yes or no answer.

Self-disclosure: She hears the question as a comment that I have seen her new hairstyle, and I don't like it.

Appeal: Tamara understands the question as a suggestion – or even a demand – to do something different – and better – with her hair.

Relationship: She hears that I liked her more when she had long hair and now my feelings for her, since she cut her hair, are not as strong as before.

My message can be understood in any of these different ways. If I want to communicate on the factual level but she hears with her relationship ear, then the misunderstanding is a foregone conclusion and the battle begins. If people do not speak the same language and are not communicating on the same level, huge misunderstandings develop that can literally end in war.

According to historical sources, the wealthy Lydian King Croesus in the sixth century BC asked the Oracle of Delphi for advice when planning to attack the Persians. The answer was, "If Croesus goes to war, he will destroy a great empire." The king liked what he heard and went head first into the battle, which turned out to be his last. As it happened, the "great empire" that would be destroyed was his own. More often than not, we only hear what we want to hear. Even when we are listening for God's voice, there is a real danger that we will not accept an undesired "no" and cling to the slightest hint of a "yes".

Everything depends on good communication – that is why God stepped in when people wanted to rise up to his level by building a tower that reached up to heaven. He made communication impossible by introducing different languages, and, thus, created a challenge to our cooperation, which continues unabated to this day. God said:

If as one people speaking the same language they have begun to do this, then nothing they plan to do will be impossible for them. Come, let us go down and confuse their language so they will not understand each other.
(Genesis 11:6–7, NIV)

If you look at it from the other side, you could say that when we are able to speak the same language and find unity, then nothing will be impossible for us. This is what the disciples experienced on Pentecost when God's Spirit came upon them. At Babel they started off speaking the same language and then suddenly could no longer understand each other, but on Pentecost, each person spoke another language and they still understood each other. I believe that there is incredible power in unity and in speaking the same language – and I'm not just talking about linguistics. This power changes our thinking and influences our culture. When we cannot find common ground in our communication, relationships suffer to the point where we can no longer continue together. But when we find a common language – as Christians, as the local church, but also in a marriage or friendship – then nothing is impossible for us. Learning to speak Newlandic is definitely worthwhile!

EXPOSING THE RELATIONSHIP NERVE

After years of suffering from chronic back pain, I got the unexpected diagnosis of a seriously herniated disc and was urgently recommended to schedule an operation as soon as possible. Although I was already experiencing symptoms like weakness down one leg, I was unaware of how close I was to having permanent damage and long-term physical impairment. After all, it was "only" back pain, like lots of other people I meet also have.

Obviously it was more serious than I had realized. My disc had given up and moved from its intended place. Now it was pressing on a large area of the nerve channel, which caused my symptoms and could eventually have led to permanent damage. It was also not comforting to hear that the prescribed operation, if unsuccessful, could result in the same long-term disability that it was intended to prevent. Suddenly, I was confronted with New Land. What if the disc moved again or if they damaged a nerve during the operation? How would I deal with life-long pain, a permanent loss of strength, or even paralysis? Had I unknowingly played my last tennis match the day before?

These are things that many other people have to come to terms with and learn to live with, but they came upon me so unexpectedly and out of the blue. Sitting in the sterile consultation room, I saw myself standing on the cusp of New Land and wondered exactly which aspect of that huge problem was the most challenging. It really didn't help when the wide-eyed doctor looked at my X-ray and said, "Wow! I've never seen such a bad one!" I had ignored all the symptoms for far too long.

The same thing can happen in a relationship. At some point things start to push and pull us and even cause us pain. But instead of examining the situation, you just keep going, thinking that everybody has those kinds of symptoms. You're right: it is normal to have problems from time to time in every relationship. But at the point where nerves are being pinched and one or both partners experience dysfunction or loss of strength, then things have become unhealthy. Very often we ignore these kinds of symptoms in our relationships for far too long, just going on as if nothing were wrong. We fail to realize that the backbone of our relationship is in danger of suffering permanent damage, so that certain areas even die off completely.

For example, over the years, you may fall into the habit of snapping at each other when it comes to a particular topic.

This disparaging approach becomes the norm. Or perhaps you develop an unconscious disdain for your partner. You choose to ignore the situation – or maybe even your partner – thinking that will be less painful for the other person. When these kinds of things start to seem normal, then the relationship nerve is under pressure and is in danger of being permanently damaged. Sometimes in this kind of situation, external help is needed from someone who can relieve the pressure, exposing the nerve like the surgeon who removed part of my slipped disc.

Tamara and I have recently had to admit that the past six or seven years with four young daughters have taken a greater toll on our marriage than we initially realized. All those sleepless nights, so many new things to think about and discuss regarding the kids, lots of stressful days with challenges, and feeling generally overwhelmed more often than not have resulted in us investing too little time in ourselves and our relationship. We simply didn't have enough energy to talk things through, and we were on the way to just coexisting. That might work as a short-term strategy, but then the time comes to step out of that rut and learn a new way. Ignorance, pride, or prior hurts should not be allowed to destroy a relationship.

It is possible – as with my back problem – that a deeper examination is necessary for one or both partners. It may be unpleasant or scary to be confronted with the diagnosis of a serious problem that you didn't really expect, but there are some situations in which external help, or perhaps even a major operation, is required. Even admitting that may be painful, not to mention what the treatment and recovery process will entail. No operation or recovery process is easy, but they usually bring healing. They make it possible for us to enjoy a relaxed, happy, healthy relationship again. And, in the long run, they open up new perspectives in life.

The thing that really concerned me about my back problem was the fact that such a little part, that tiny disc, could put my whole body out of commission if it wasn't in its proper place. It presses on the nerve, and in the worst case, everything below that point could stop functioning altogether. I had ignored that pressure on the nerve and the pain it caused for too long. For me, this is a clear illustration of what happens in God's kingdom. As Christians, we are called Christ's body. This body can also have problems when one part moves from its intended position. It gets on our nerves. It is unpleasant and we feel the pressure. That's exactly where we need to start looking. We cannot stay silent when something is putting pressure on a nerve. If we ignore it, the pain will spread and affect the entire body.

How are you feeling the pressure in your marriage or in relationship with other Christians? Where have you fled into "survival mode" and never come out?

In what areas have you let a small annoyance slip out of place to the extent that it may cause permanent damage or a complete loss of function?

Ask God to restore your "slipped disc" back to the correct position. Be sure to do your physical therapy exercises – like "forgiveness squats" or "taking the initiative push-ups" – to help your relationship recover and heal. Please don't be afraid of getting external help in the process.

Since my slipped disc episode, I have read the following Bible verse a bit differently: "The eye cannot say to the hand, 'I don't need you!' And the head cannot say to the feet, 'I don't need you!' On the contrary, those parts of the body that seem to be weaker are indispensable" (1 Corinthians 12:21–22, NIV).

This is why Christian unity is in such bad shape. When we allow ourselves to have negative thoughts about other Christians, denominations, or traditions, we are saying – or maybe just thinking – "I don't need you." We ignore, belittle, or question certain aspects of their faith, perhaps even denying that they have any faith at all. It starts with gossiping about others and avoiding cooperation. Things develop in a one-sided way because there is nothing to balance us out or no other point of view to consider. Pain and paralysis are the result, but, most of all, we block God's promised blessing. If we would only act in the opposite way – speaking well of one another and standing together – then a climate of cooperation develops and we feel its power. We can learn to see others through God's eyes and live in Newlandic relationships.

This is why God decided to restore broken relationships through Christ. First and foremost, it is about our relationship to him, and after that it is about our relationships with other people. It is not just "the others" who need to hear this message; it starts with you and me. In Matthew 9:12 (CEV), Jesus says, "Healthy people don't need a doctor, but sick people do."

I really hope that we can stop ignoring this painful pressure that results in paralysis and loss of strength in God's kingdom and begin to accept it so that we can allow God, who is the best possible physician, to operate and restore. This will result in his body – we Christians – being able to run at full speed as we make Christ visible in our healthy relationships. The Relationship Territory awaits, and unity is an important part of it.

7

IDYLLIC
The Unity Territory

The Unity Territory is a particular area within the Relationship Territory of New Land. I have experienced my most significant growth steps in recent years through Christians from other faith traditions and from different backgrounds to my own. We have so much to offer one another; our faith horizons are broadened through contact with others. The kingdom of God is so much larger than the church or denomination to which we belong. In heaven, things will be idyllic as we sit next to each other – surely it is better to start practising here on earth.

I often hear arguments from different sides – some understandable, others less so – as to why the beliefs of the other side are more wrong than right. At that point the peaceful ideal flies out the window. Over the years, I have begun to suspect that the Christ we all lay claim to is playing in a completely different league from us, his followers, in terms of his mercy, broad perspective, and generosity. That's probably what caused Mahatma Gandhi, the head of the Indian independence movement, to rightly remark, "I like your Christ. I do not like your Christians. Your Christians are so unlike your Christ."

Our faith and personal concept of truth are much more closely linked to our personal stories than we realize. And many aspects of other people's faith can bother us or even seem wrong when we are unable to fit them into our own personal background and culture. We always need to be aware of the fact that our perceptions are only partial, and, even as believers, we will never be able to completely grasp God – just like a group of blind people trying to comprehend an elephant. Each of them feels what is in front of them, trying to describe what an elephant is like from feeling only an ear, a tusk, the trunk, a leg, or the tail. When they share their experiences later, it is not surprising that the individual versions of what an elephant is like would be vastly different. Each of them had examined the elephant closely and described it accurately – but from very different perspectives; each one is limited by his or her scope of experience. In the same way, our faith is a subjective truth based on what we have experienced and understood to the best of our ability. It is good to admit to yourself that you are only able to examine a small part of the whole animal.

My encounters with Christians from a wide range of denominations and traditions have taught me so much. Things that used to annoy have been resolved because now I understand the logic behind that belief. Other things have remained irritating, and that's OK, too. Walking together does not mean that we all have to believe in the same way. I don't have to agree with everything or understand everything, and I can still feel that some things are wrong. Even though I have known Tamara for nearly two decades now, we still disagree on some things. And sometimes we just can't understand how it is possible for us to perceive the same thing so very differently. But we also realize that we do not have to agree on every point in order to love one another. And this is the foundation upon which unity grows.

The goal cannot be for us to see everything in the same way and to create a wishy-washy faith in order to be as unified as possible. I am not in favour of an all-reconciling, one world religion. Instead, it should be about striving for unity in our core values and refraining from condemning one another with regard to personal opinions on secondary subjects or our own pet topics. It can be helpful to examine ourselves critically and, perhaps, to realize that Jesus would sometimes emphasize topics aside from the ones that we are particularly passionate about.

A lot of rejection is based on personal faith preferences, primarily out of fear of what is different or out of ignorance. Wherever people have to move beyond their pride and overcome their own entrenched opinions, there is a real possibility for people to have authentic, deep encounters with one another, characterized by respect and love. This is the Newlandic location where moments of understanding, knowledge, and growth – because of and with one another – start to take place, regardless of whatever else is visible.

A while ago, the global internet community was divided over the colour of a particular dress in a photo. Was it blue and black or white and gold? I looked at that photo on the monitor in my office and I wondered what the point of all this nonsense was. It looked blue and black to me. Imagine my surprise when I surveyed my office colleagues, and about half of them were convinced that the dress was white and gold. I thought I was going mad! Then I saw the endless list of comments under the photo that continued the 50/50 disagreement, and I learned that we all perceive colours differently depending on how our brains process the surroundings, like shadows. It works the same way with faith. Things that seem completely clear to you, to the point that you cannot understand how anyone could see them otherwise, may not be all that clear to someone else – it often depends on personal perception.

Often a broad and open approach to working with other denominations is rejected based on the idea that there is something wrong with the other's faith and that we know and must protect the complete truth – at least the truth as we see it. But so much of what we do in the name of "protecting the faith" is really nothing more than a lack of love in a devout disguise.

In John 12, when a woman generously – perhaps even wastefully – anointed Jesus with a jar of oil that would have cost as much as an annual salary, Judas' comments about the cost seemed legitimate: perhaps the money would have been better spent on the poor (John 12:5). But that woman had used that oil to express her love for Jesus, and he knew how to acknowledge her gift. Love is a gift that is always extravagant, even wasteful. And, although Judas' objection sounds logical and God-focused, it actually lacks love and reveals his true heart. He calls oil worth 300 silver coins a waste, but he later sells out his friend Jesus for a mere thirty pieces of silver.

Again and again I am shocked to see that in places where God's love ought to be visible, I get slapped in the face with rejection, exclusion, and unkindness – all out of a conviction that God's truth is being protected and that people will be held in check as long as someone holds that value high and sets clear boundaries so that faith cannot be denied. No one wants to be assaulted by that rooster crowing three times in their ear. But no matter how you look at it, in the end, well-meaning attempts to preserve and protect must often be seen as evidence of a lack of love. We find ourselves walking in the footsteps of Saul, who was convinced of his divine mission, but was utterly misguided in his zeal.

Be honest: do you have a "them and us" attitude? What are your arguments against them? When you examine your thinking carefully, what reasons can you find for your attitudes or opinions? What are you afraid of? What foundation are those attitudes built on? (You may need to go back and read the chapter about fear.)

Often our most defensive reactions are in areas where we could afford to be stretched a bit. Perhaps you find yourself annoyed that others are too ___ (insert your own adjective), or you find their behaviour or beliefs "dodgy" or even "dangerous". Perhaps you need to grow in this area yourself.

Relax and enjoy the ideal of diversity, without having to give up your critical thinking skills.

At the end of the day, there is still a handful of things I experience but cannot understand, maybe even some things I find completely wrong. But I think God can handle that dissonance just fine.

THE KEY TO UNITY

The key to unity is not having an identical faith but sharing the same Spirit. I always appreciate those special moments when I have been able to come together to pray with Christians from different backgrounds and feel that same Spirit that unites us. It is not important whether we all express our faith in the same way, but that we are connected on a deeper, inner level. If God's Spirit lives in both me and my neighbour, then this becomes the basis for our cooperation, in spite of debates or differences of opinion on certain issues. God's Spirit does not battle against himself. If a fight happens, then it is always a result of human dynamics. We need to develop an attitude of generosity toward diversity and learn to enjoy the process of finding common ground.

In my experience, the best opportunities for cooperation are those where no single theological point or particular form of faith is allowed to take centre stage. Instead, everyone chooses to keep Christ at the centre and move forward together, in the power of the Holy Spirit. As long as Christ is leading the way (John 14:6), we can always find a path of cooperation with his help.

Psalm 133:1, 3 (TPT) say, "How truly wonderful and delightful to see brothers and sisters living together in sweet unity! This heavenly harmony can be compared to the dew dripping down from the skies upon Mount Hermon, refreshing the mountain slopes of Israel. For from this realm of sweet harmony God will release his eternal blessing, the promise of life forever!" "Sweet harmony" means a friendly coexistence, and that has nothing to do with everyone thinking, believing, or feeling exactly the same. Instead, it is about adopting a positive attitude toward the other person, even when we approach things in different ways. When we are united with our fellow believers, then God can't help but bless us – he has promised to do just that.

I just love tearing down walls of separation and using the old stones to build new bridges that unite us. I do my best to be a world-class speaker of blessing to others and search passionately for what unites in order to overcome whatever threatens to keep us separate from one another.

When I recently spoke at a Catholic event, I was deeply moved at the reverence of the Eucharist (the Lord's Supper). I discovered a new aspect of God's holiness that I hadn't felt in other church services. I still have a lot of questions, but instead of allowing myself to get annoyed over those differences, I have learned to explore this New Land with curiosity and a heart that looks for the best in people and situations. At the same time, I don't pressure myself to participate in every aspect or to agree and believe everything. The goal is to be able to talk with one another about the things we do not understand in the hope of learning something new and expanding our horizon of knowledge and faith.

Choosing to have an open mind and approaching situations without fear allows us to break down prejudices and learn to discern real concerns from exaggerations. Many of the following ideas come from my wise friend and office partner, Peter. They all apply to the tension that often exists between Catholics and evangelical Protestants. Some of the points also apply to the relationships to other churches and denominations, from charismatics to Orthodox.

It is always good to ponder the topic of unity in our hearts and in prayer and to thank God for things that impress and inspire us (or, in Newlandic terminology, things that stretch us), but we can also admit when things remain odd, off-putting, or even seem wrong to us.

The most important thing is to be able to distinguish between the inner processes and outward expressions of our faith. This means that we can learn to differentiate between the inward connection with God and the outward forms of expression or the paths of faith we or our counterparts take. It is essential that we learn to transfer outward expressions and practices to the inner life and not the other way around. The inward self naturally seeks outward forms to express itself and to develop. These outward expressions are also an important way to preserve the inner life and to bring others into our fellowships. However, outward expression should not take precedence over the inner process, despite the fact that the inner life and its practices are often closely intertwined with outward expressions. It is still important to remind ourselves repeatedly that unity does not grow out of shared practices and forms of expression but out of a shared inner faith, regardless of exactly how that faith is lived out.

In Romans 14, Paul writes about how to deal with dietary laws. He mentions some principles that can help us in working together with other denominations.

> *Welcome all the Lord's followers, even those whose faith is weak. Don't criticize them for having beliefs that are different from yours. Some think it is all right to eat anything, while those whose faith is weak will eat only vegetables.*
> (Romans 14: 1–2, CEV)

We can read this text through a Catholic lens that sees the Protestant as the one whose "faith is weak", or vice versa. The bottom line is that we should accept one another without arguing about different views on certain issues.

> *The one who eats freely shouldn't judge and look down on the one who eats only vegetables. And the vegetarian must not judge and look down on the one who eats everything. Remember, God has welcomed him and taken him as his partner.*
> (Romans 14:3, TPT)

Although this example focuses on misunderstood freedoms with regard to food and drink, you could easily apply it to the Eucharist and say, "Whoever eats meat (Catholics believe that the bread becomes the body of Christ) should not look down on the one who does not eat meat (or who does not share the same Catholic doctrinal understanding). In the same way, evangelicals and Protestants should not judge their Catholic brothers and sisters."

> *Why do you criticize other followers of the Lord? Why do you look down on them? The day is coming when God will judge all of us.*
> (Romans 14:10, CEV)

Paul reminds us here of the personal responsibility of every believer before Jesus.

> *We must stop judging others. We must also make up our minds not to upset anyone's faith. The Lord Jesus has made it clear to me that God considers all foods fit to eat. But if you think some foods are unfit to eat, then for you they are not fit. If you are hurting others by the foods you eat, you are not guided by love. Don't let your appetite destroy someone Christ died for. Don't let your right to eat bring shame to Christ.*
> (Romans 14:13–16, CEV)

We need to be careful not to confuse or upset our brothers and sisters through our outward expressions of faith (or our own understanding of them).

> *God's kingdom isn't about eating and drinking. It is about pleasing God, about living in peace, and about true happiness. All this comes from the Holy Spirit. If you serve Christ in this way, you will please God and be respected by people.*
> (Romans 14:17–18, CEV)

In God's kingdom (and in terms of the unity among those who belong to that kingdom) it's not really about outward things like eating or not eating, but rather about the inner process of faith, a shared experience of the Holy Spirit and his righteousness, peace, and joy.

> *We should try to live at peace and help each other have a strong faith. Don't let your appetite destroy what God has done. All foods are fit to eat, but it is wrong to cause problems for others by what you eat.*
> (Romans 14:19–20, CEV)

This means that outward expressions of faith can actually become obstacles to unity when we try to force others to adopt them, or when our own freedom in a particular area causes another to stumble., In short, I respect others, and I refrain when necessary; I live according to my own understanding and convictions, but I remain engaged with others. It is possible for a diverse group of Christians to have complete spiritual unity even without our own individual "holy" forms of expression.

The most important factors are how alive and contagious the other person's love for God and their neighbour is, the fervour of their worship, and the intensity of their inner fire. However, we need to be careful not to measure these qualities based on our own specific faith expressions, no matter how dear they are to us. If we do, there will certainly be friction with others. It is always good to realize and reflect on our own one-sidedness. That is why engaging with Christians from other denominations is so important. Still, we should always "[try our] best to let God's Spirit keep [our] hearts united" (Ephesians 4:3, CEV).

In short, being able to affirm the faith of people who believe in Jesus in ways that go beyond the boundaries of our own congregation or denomination and conceding that they also have deep, meaningful experiences with God regardless of whether or not they share our same forms and expressions of faith is the best way to reduce the tension and stress that often exists. After all, we shouldn't judge ourselves or others as "better" or "more correct" in faith.

The image of family has been so helpful to me in this process, especially when I think about the typical stress that accompanies family Christmas gatherings. Consider this example: everyone looks forward to being together, but it is always difficult to fit everything in during the holiday season. When you finally get everybody together, old behaviour patterns quickly emerge. Some realize quickly that, despite the love they have for their relatives, they can't stand to be together for long periods of time. Family is just unbearable. But it is also unbearably wonderful. It's the same way in God's family. You know that you belong together because you share the same heavenly Father, maybe you even try to get together from time to time, but at some point you are confronted with all the annoying stuff that goes with every family encounter. (Just in case any of my relatives ever reads this book, let me assure you that this doesn't apply to you – our family is completely different. You never annoy me, and I love you more than you know!)

Where do you have opportunities to engage with Christians from other churches or denominations? What have your experiences been like so far?

Ultimately, in a world where so many relationships are struggling to survive, I believe that unity serves as powerful evidence of God's existence. Jesus put it this way in the prayer he prayed for us:

I want all of them to be one with each other, just as I am one with you and you are one with me. I also want them to be one with us. Then the people of this world will believe that you sent me. I have honoured my followers in the same way that you honoured me, in order that they may be one with each other, just as we are one. I am one with them, and you are one with me, so that they may become completely one. Then this world's people will know that you sent me. They will know that you love my followers as much as you love me.

(John 17:21–23, CEV)

We make such an effort to give people around us the opportunity to encounter Christ. And that's a great thing. But, in this passage, Jesus speaks clearly about the impact of unity: when we come together as Christians, the world will see and believe. The best efforts are ineffectual and hard to believe when churches and congregations are battling one another.

Once I asked a friend of mine why he didn't believe in Jesus. His answer was absolutely clear: "Just look at how your churches treat one another. Bring all these churches together, and then I'll consider believing." So that guy, who doesn't believe in God, had figured out something that we Christians often fail to understand. Our actions speak louder than all our sermons combined.

It is inspiring to realize that we live in a time in which God is shaping this unity in new ways. Networks of Christians are springing up at an exciting rate. Believers from disparate backgrounds are more and more willing to put greater emphasis on what unites over what separates us, as long as Christ remains in the centre. God is opening up New Land for us, and the question is whether you are ready to go down this new path and to discover new territory with a humble awareness that many others have already gone down that path before you.

Where do you have opportunities to meet with your Newlandic family? Are outward expressions still preventing you from engaging with others? How?

THE WAR IS OVER

I often meet people who stand in their own way and block their path into New Land. This always reminds me of the verse from Jeremiah 4:3, "Break up your unploughed ground and do not sow among thorns" (NIV). They fail to enter New Land in their own faith because they have allowed a thorn bush of worries and fears to grow. There are also a few thorn bushes of prejudices toward other Christians that they can't get rid of because these thorny shrubs keep everyone else at such a distance that there is never even a chance to get close to someone from the other group. The worst offenders, though, are the tall hedgerows of pride that enable us to simply ignore whomever or whatever is on the other side. Our view becomes limited; we are unable to see the diversity in God's huge garden, his kingdom.

What we often fail to realize is that our attitudes of rejection, self-protection, or even plain ignorance not only keep us at arms' length from fellow believers, but they block our view of the New Land God intends for us. We make ourselves comfortable in Old Land because ploughing a new field always means effort and sweat.

In what areas is it time for you to leave Old Land behind and to enter New Land? What thorns are keeping new things from growing?

The Preacher to the Papal Household, Father Raniero Cantalamessa, a good friend of mine, invited me to the Vatican and offered me the opportunity to meet the Pope himself. I knew that such a meeting would not please everyone, but some of the comments I received after posting a photo on Facebook and also in letters crossed all boundaries of good taste. The way people talked about other Christian denominations revealed haughty hearts out of which flowed rivers of unkindness. It's a frightening reality, especially when you consider that God's love is supposed to be made visible to the world through us. The unloving attitudes that fly in my face and the overdose of moral superiority that comes from within our own ranks are far more destructive than whatever those people are objecting to. The German writer Johann Paul Friedrich Richter is credited with the statement "You always hear about people who have lost their minds for the sake of love. But there are also many who have lost love for the sake of their minds." So many people try to cement their faith in such rigidly correct terms that they fail to realize that their love for others has fallen off the wagon somewhere along the way. And without love, what are we left with?

If I were to speak with eloquence in earth's many languages, and in the heavenly tongues of angels, yet I didn't express myself with love, my words would be reduced to the hollow sound of nothing more than a clanging cymbal. And if I were to have the gift of prophecy

> *with a profound understanding of God's hidden secrets, and if I possessed unending supernatural knowledge, and if I had the greatest gift of faith that could move mountains, but have never learned to love, then I am nothing. And if I were to be so generous as to give away everything I owned to feed the poor, and to offer my body to be burned as a martyr, without the pure motive of love, I would gain nothing of value. Until then, there are three things that remain: faith, hope, and love – yet love surpasses them all.*

(1 Corinthians 13:1–3, 13, TPT)

Without love, even our best efforts are not only worthless, they become the exact opposite of what they were intended for. Unfortunately, these results can often be seen in the flood of inappropriate and negative comments that typically collect at the end of a Facebook post. I have even received disparaging videos about other Christians that claim to uncover vast conspiracies involving almost any Christian leader or cutting-edge revival movement you can think of. Have you ever realized that the ones who never make a visible impact don't have any opponents? If there is nothing controversial happening in your church, and if no one is proposing conspiracy theories about your denomination, then perhaps that should make you a bit nervous.

Naturally, any genuine spiritual revival is usually accompanied by rather strange human excesses. However, branding a revival or an entire movement as negative would be like deciding not to marry your dream woman because you found out that she likes to eat Nutella, pickles, and rhubarb on toast as a snack.

We all need to learn to be a bit more courageous, to look at things with an open mind and through the filter of love without throwing the baby out with the bathwater, and then, out of pure desperation, try to scratch off the enamel in the bathtub with our fingernails.

During my first visit to the Vatican, Father Raniero preached an impressive sermon to the Pope and about seventy Catholic leaders on the topic of unity and cooperation between Protestants and Catholics. In that sermon, he told the story of Hiroo Onoda, a soldier in World War II who never heard the news of Japan's surrender. He was on one of the 7,641 islands that make up the Philippines and the news just never made it there. All attempts to get him to give up failed. He even suspected that flyers sent to him from his own family were a trick of the enemy. After the war officially ended in 1945, Hiroo continued to fight on his own for twenty-nine more years. In that time, he killed thirty people and injured more than one hundred others. It wasn't until 1974, when one of his former commanding officers managed to contact him, that Hiroo agreed to stop fighting. He was still wearing his uniform and had hand grenades and other ammunition. Against the backdrop of this story, Father Raniero announced to his listeners, "The war is over." Like Hiroo, many Christians have never heard this message.

In what areas are you still fighting against other Christians or anyone else? Against a neighbour? Against foreigners or immigrants? Against people with different opinions from yours? Against your spouse? Or ultimately, maybe against God, yourself, or your own fears…?

Please, put down your weapons and stop fighting. War always leads to destruction and devastation. The recoil from your own weapon may end up hurting you more than the enemy you're shooting at.

Football is seen as a game that brings people together, but often it has exactly the opposite effect. During the qualifiers for the 1970 World Cup, Honduras played against El Salvador. The deciding third match on 26 June 1969 in Mexico City ended with a score of 3–2 for El Salvador after extra time, putting Honduras out of the tournament. The result was the so-called "Football War", which left 2,100 people dead and 6,000 casualties. Ultimately, it was not just about a lost football match but was a question of national identity. Honduras had been flooded with Salvadorans over the years, and the Hondurans perceived them as unwelcome intruders in their country.[20]

In "wars" between denominations, the battle is not always about the most obvious point of contention, but something deeper. We allow ourselves to be driven by a false identity. Our primary identity is not Catholic or Protestant, Pentecostal, non-denominational, Anglican, Orthodox, Salvation Army, or whatever else you can think of. Out identity is in Christ himself. When we lose this point of reference and give preference to our denominational identity, then we have already dug the trenches.

The greatest characteristic of Jesus is not that he is a military leader, but that he is the Prince of Peace. This has a concrete impact on our personal lives and leads us into the fifth Newlandic Territory that we as Christians should discover.

8

HERO
IC

The World Territory

The heavenly kingdom has different values and a different culture to the world around us, which we cannot expect from our environment or set as a standard. But we can live in a Newlandic way and become a fragrant aroma. Since we do not go through life as solitary travellers, every relationship presents an opportunity to make an impact; either we shape our situation, or it shapes us.

For many years, I always sat in the restaurant carriage as I travelled to work by train. There was a server there who was almost always overwhelmed by her situation. Either you didn't get what you ordered, or sometimes you didn't get anything at all. And no matter what came, it was always served with a negative comment or at least a frown. On one particular journey, I got pulled into her negative spiral. I had boarded the train in my usual merry mood – well, as merry as one can be in the morning – only to arrive in Zurich an hour later feeling agitated, sour, and ready to pounce on anybody who got too close. Then and there, I decided that I would not allow myself to be clouded by that negative energy ever again. A battle cry took shape in my mind: "I will shape my environment!"

Right now, many people are anxiously wondering how the world has got so messed up, how things will turn out in Europe, when the financial system will finally collapse, where the next war will break out, how we should view globalization, where today's almost constant surveillance will lead us, how we will survive the ongoing flood of refugees, where all the talk about gender will end, what the decline of values means, and where the growing suspicion of all things Christian will take us. Our entire society seems to be saturated with worry, fear, and a strong sense of doom and gloom.

Sometimes it seems like the only place where people are not suffering from fear is where ignorance has already taken over. Whether intentionally or not, a strong sense of hopelessness is being stirred up as multiple economic sectors feed on the dissatisfaction and fear in society. Because people are worried, they take out insurance, try to stay up to date with the newest gadgets, and spend money to be part of the "in crowd". People do not invest money to make themselves feel hopeful, but instead to feel happy or secure. The first question many ask themselves is "What's in it for me?" Many Christians allow themselves to be carried away by sheer apathetic frustration paired with a nice shot of egotism.

But the truth is that God is not finished with the planet. He is not through with humanity. God's work in Europe is not complete. And God is not finished with you, either. That brings us a lot of hope. The God who makes all things new is still here. He cannot deny himself, and that is why New Land leads into more New Land.

And that is exactly the message of the gospel; it is first and foremost a message of hope. With God, New Land awaits. No matter how scorched the earth of your Old Land is, God has prepared New Land for you. "Is anything too hard for the Lord?" (Genesis 18:14a, NIV). There is still so much to experience and discover. Our greatest defeats happen when we stop reaching out for what God has prepared for us.

"For we are God's handiwork, created in Christ Jesus to do good works, which God prepared in advance for us to do" (Ephesians 2:10, NIV). God has placed wonderful things for us in our New Land, but as soon as we sit down and stop pursuing them, we miss out on the blessing.

When the lottery organizers write to you to say that your ticket has won the jackpot and you have four weeks to present your ticket and claim the £32 million in prize money, you would never allow yourself to miss that deadline. Instead, you would turn your house upside down to find the ticket, because you can't remember where you put it. Many Christians appear not to care where their heavenly lottery ticket actually is. Such lifeless Christianity and stiff, immovable faith not only worsens many social problems, but is often the cause. Because examples of living faith are no longer visible or tangible, society moves steadily into hopelessness. However, a Newlandic culture is the foundation for a Christianity that pulsates with life and provides fertile soil for living faith to grow. Unfortunately, many Christians are led astray by their fears and insecurities and end up creating their own enemies to fight against.

As Christians, we already have our heavenly citizenship and are empowered to make heavenly culture visible here on earth. More than anything else, we need to reach out to catch a glimpse of God's kingdom and let it take shape in our lives.

Shape your world by moving into New Land.

YOUR ROLE AS PEACEMAKER

"Blessed are the peacemakers, for they will be called children of God" (Matthew 5:9, NIV). This verse came to life in a special way on 24 December 1914 during the midst of fighting in World War I.[21] After many soldiers enthusiastically went off to war, the initial euphoria gradually evaporated as it became clear they would not be home for Christmas. In Flanders, soldiers were literally opposite each other in open trenches that had become icy mud holes in the bad winter weather. After five months, the western front was nearly paralysed with soldiers sobered by the high number of dead, the lack of ammunition, and the dwindling prospect of a quick victory. Pope Benedict XV had expressed the desire to see a Christmas truce, but both sides had refused.

Some 355,000 Christmas parcels had been sent to British soldiers with the king's blessing. The Germans also received many private parcels and tens of thousands of miniature Christmas trees at the front. As Christmas approached, both sides felt a growing desire for peace and the opportunity to open their gifts with the security of a truce.

In some places, the trenches were only separated by 50 to 100 metres, allowing the troops to speak freely with one another. One English war correspondent described how, instead of the usual grenades, the Germans threw a chocolate cake into the no man's land between the two sides, which the British gladly received. People recounted how the Germans sang Christmas songs and the British applauded their performance. The Brits also sang, and the Germans responded by setting up a couple of their Christmas trees on the edge of their trench. On the morning of 24 December, most sectors were calm. Soldiers called out to the other side to announce that they wanted to recover the fallen from no man's land, and no one shot as both sides collected their comrades. While they were out, the men began to speak to one another. At one point, the British were given two kegs of beer, and they returned the favour by passing over some Christmas puddings. Near the village of Fromelles, people from both sides gathered on an 80-metre-wide swathe of no man's land to celebrate a Christmas service together in which they recited Psalm 23. Many diaries and reports paint the picture that these moments were wonderfully surreal for the participants: an unbelievable experience surrounded by an air of magical mystery. You can read of many Christmas celebrations between the warring factions: there was at least one pig roast, the men offered to shave one another and give each other haircuts, they shared family photos, played several football matches, and exchanged small gifts like tobacco, cigarettes, and chocolate. The magic of the season unfolded with a simple, disarming power and led to unplanned fraternization. The reason? Christmas! The day the Prince of Peace was born made peace in this world possible again: peace with God, with other people, and with ourselves.

It truly requires great courage to stand up for peace and to advocate for it. As you raise your head above the parapet, you don't know whether your offer of peace and open hand extended to the other side will be accepted or refused. You don't know whether to expect a cake or bullets flying your way. But this is exactly what we are called to do: to leave our trenches, to put up and decorate Christmas trees on their edges, and to approach the people on the other side with open arms.

Anyone who is not prepared to take steps into the no man's land of New Land will automatically succumb to the temptation to defend only their Old Land. Then come trench battles that only result in death, never gaining one metre of territory. We have been called to be peacemakers and should do everything in our power to make peace possible. The reaction from the other side is beyond our control.

A few months ago, I stumbled upon a verse that has stayed with me: "When peacemakers plant seeds of peace, they will harvest justice" (James 3:18, CEV). I have been tasked by God to work for peace and to plant seeds of justice. The most wonderful thing about this assignment is not just the task itself, but the fact that I am empowered to do these things at all. In any everyday situation, I can choose how to react. And especially when I feel I have been treated inappropriately, I still always have the choice of whether I want to sow seeds of peace or of war. It's as if God has put seeds of peace in my right pocket, but I fill my left pocket with seeds of war. Far too often I allow myself to be persuaded to sow a seed of war instead of a seed of peace. Those war seeds never bring good fruit; rather, they suck the life out of everything around and bring death. The result is unhealthy, dysfunctional, and dead relationships.

But what if we actually took the challenge to be peacemakers to heart? Practically, it might look like this: put something in your right pocket that will remind you of the "seeds of peace", maybe a couple of sweets. Any time you get tripped up during the day, maybe by your spouse, that stupid driver in the car in front of you, or perhaps your eccentric work colleague, then think about those seeds of peace. You can't change people or situations, but it's up to you which seed you sow in response, depending on which fruit you hope to harvest out of your life and relationships. Every time you succeed in sowing a seed of peace, reward yourself with a sweet. Your goal is to get rid of all the sweets by the end of the day.

During a visit to the UN in Geneva, I met a man from Ghana. He was an unremarkable, small man who had been highly praised by everyone there, which made me very curious. His story is as moving as any Hollywood script. He was a simple bookkeeper working for the UN in an entry-level position. Late one evening in July 2003, he came across a cheque that he had issued himself, but on which the recipient's name had been changed. He was suspicious and continued looking. In the end, he found twenty-five cheques totalling some $400,000. When he tried to share this with his boss, he was turned away and told to butt out. He kept knocking on leaders' doors and was turned away again and again. No one wanted him to keep sniffing around, and people threatened to fire him; he even received anonymous threats. But this man from Ghana believed in Christ and lived according to his Christian convictions and values. He did not stop telling the truth until he found someone who would listen. This proved to be one of the largest UN scandals ever. Over a number of years, someone had siphoned off more than US$3 million. The story made it into *The New York Times*, and many key people were forced to leave their jobs.

Shortly thereafter, the search for a new financial director began. A man of integrity who could be trusted was chosen to fill the position: that inconspicuous man from Ghana. Meeting him and hearing his story touched me. I was impressed by his courage to stand up and fight for peace. He had decided not to sit back and watch as others sowed seeds of injustice and war. He was able to bring peace into a global organization through his courage and integrity. The fruit can still be seen today.

You are a peacemaker. Where do you see war and strife around you or in your own life? How could you take a courageous stand and choose to sow peace in those situations? Or what concrete step can you take instead of just looking away?

When you consider the different areas of your life – your neighbours, your marriage, your church, your workplace,

your friends, your teammates – where do you find yourself sowing the wrong seeds too often?

THE DRAMA ON EASTER ISLAND

The result of sowing strife instead of Newlandic peace can be seen in the dramatic and brutal history of the tribes on Easter Island. There are many myths and theories surrounding them, but one very plausible tale has captivated me. When that isolated island, which spans 163.6 km^2 and is completely unprotected from wind and weather, was rediscovered in the South Pacific, people found huge stone figures all over the island – heads and bodies up to 21 metres tall and weighing on average 12.5 tonnes. Initially, these stone heads must have stood upright, but their back story was surrounded by mystery.

Previously, the island had been divided into eleven districts, each with its own chief. We assume that the chiefs erected the stone figures as status symbols or signs of their power. The figures grew larger and larger over time, as proven by the unfinished figures still lying in the island's quarry. Re-enactments have shown that the largest figures would have needed some 500 men, probably an entire tribe, to pull them into position. Large wooden beams and ropes made from trees that grew on the island were needed to transport them. At some point, all the trees had been cut down, the proof of which can be found in the deposits in firepits around the island. On the bottom, they found the bones of dolphins, which could only be caught out in the open ocean, far from the island. Over time, these bones disappeared. The islanders must eventually have run out of large trees with which to build their sea-faring canoes, and could not erect any more stone figures. So they began knocking down the other tribes' stone figures. At some point, there was no more firewood available, and people had to burn plant waste and ferns. The lack of trees on the island meant it was even more vulnerable to the tides and storms, eventually making all farming impossible.

The fate of an entire civilization was thus sealed. All fishhooks disappeared from the firepits – in the upper layers the remains of rats and human bones were found, revealing a dramatic conclusion in cannibalism. An island that had been home to perhaps 17,500 inhabitants died out because people, blinded by their lust for power, had destroyed their own livelihood.

Scientists draw conclusions about our own global society from this self-contained island system. Society's behaviour today is exactly the same; many people strive for power, seeking to fulfil their own agenda. They build their own kingdoms, always looking out for number one. Today we don't erect huge stone figures to impress others, but it is perfectly normal for our cars to get bigger and bigger. Or maybe our houses. Perhaps it's about achieving a higher position at work, in the church, or in politics; maybe it's the newest smartphone, more followers on Instagram, an expensive watch, or a well-padded bank account.

Where leadership stops serving, the maelstrom of self-destruction starts to churn. Instead of sowing peace, we insist on raising our own position and yearn to have the biggest stone figure. Instead of humbly learning to reach out to others and live together on that island, we fight for our own advantage, power, and territory, and these things hinder life.

When leaders follow their pride and their own advantage instead of shaping the world with Newlandic culture, they pull everyone and everything down with them. In general, pursuing personal agendas first and being unwilling to reach out to others, allowing marriages and other relationships to die slow deaths, and the destruction of unity among Christians are all ways of sowing war, not peace.

You have been called to be a peacemaker, not the chief! Where have you put up stone figures for yourself?

In what situations can you see traces of unhealthy pride in yourself? Perhaps a lust for power? A dissatisfaction over what others have and you do not?

Where are you sometimes overcome with jealousy? Where can you see manipulative tendencies in yourself that draw people into things that do not promote peace? Where have you stopped spreading a pleasing aroma of New Land?

It is not our own kingdom that is important, but God's. I became very aware of this when I started preaching and the stages I stood on quickly became bigger and bigger. So I adopted a prayer ritual from my very first attempts at preaching. Before I go onto the stage, I always pray, "Heavenly Father, please expand your kingdom and not mine." We should not be concerned with building our own kingdoms, but the kingdom of God that he chooses to make visible through us as we actively engage with the world around us and seek to shape it on all levels. Making peace is only one aspect. The World Territory contains many aspects, from social justice to politics, economics and business, practical help, and even bearing witness in word and deed to the ways that Jesus is at work in and around us.

Where are you secretly building your own kingdom? Or where are you following people who are focused on building their own kingdoms? How can you contribute to building God's kingdom in the world?

You stand on your own two feet in your own world, and the main question is not what that world is like, but, instead, how you will stand out and where you will stand up in your world. Will you shape your world, or will you let it shape you? You can make a difference.

9

MAGIC

The Newlandic Spirit

We choose some of the New Land that lies before us: I chose my profession; I decided to get married; I planned to have four children with my wife, Tamara – something that is almost unheard of today in Switzerland. When you have the first one, people congratulate you euphorically, and there is a big party. When the second one comes along, people say, "That's great, but so soon!" When the third arrives, you get a lot of confused looks and the unmistakable message "Whoops! Was this really planned?" And when you are expecting the fourth, you get a mixture of sympathy ("Are they all yours?") and shock ("How could they?!"). But when we were on sabbatical in the Philippines, everyone asked, "Four kids? ONLY four kids?" In Switzerland, I couldn't even make an appointment for us at the passport office as a family; we were considered a "group".

As we reflect on decisions and the New Land that we can intentionally steer ourselves toward, I think of how I left my secure and well-paid job as a teacher to become a missionary and preacher living off donations. In my diary at the time, I wrote down my questions and doubts: "Will anybody even want to listen to me?" That was truly New Land. It was also New Land when we made the decision to share a house with another family, to pool our resources, and live as a witness for Christ in our local community through the visible partnership between our two families. And now, we have entered New Land again with the same friends – another family with four kids – by moving to a completely different region of Switzerland in order to be closer to the office and the airport. I have also learned to speak English despite my language phobias, and I have been working for quite a while to cross over my personal boundary into the land of decent French.

Often we also face New Land in our lives in areas we have not chosen: an emergency operation, an unexpected death, getting fired, a broken relationship, a failed exam, or an unfulfilled dream. The question is never *whether* New Land will come, but *when* – followed by how we will respond to the new situation and whether or not we will accept it as a growth opportunity.

I have already written that I'm actually a bit of a home bird. I was in the avalanche troop in the military, and we often went on ski tours (climbing up the mountain wearing special trekking skis and then skiing down on virgin slopes) – they always say that the view from the summit is worth all the effort of getting there. Climbing to the top of a mountain that could have been reached much more easily by cable car just never made sense to me. And don't start talking to me about the "beauty of nature" or the "endorphin rush after physical exertion".

But despite my "take the easy route" approach to most things, I have come to understand that the magic in life – things that are extraordinary and indescribable – always happens outside my comfort zone. Only when I follow Peter out onto the water

Your comfort zone

Where the magic happens

will I have the chance to experience one of those unforgettable moments of being carried.

Because I am quite set in my ways – or perhaps in spite of that – I have made a point of integrating the New Land factor firmly into my life and of adopting a Newlandic spirit.

Every year I try to inject a new idea or concept into the system at Campus für Christus: something that brings us out of balance, forcing us to take a step forward. Just because you don't like something doesn't mean it won't help you.

How can you become a person who embraces New Land? What would bring you out of balance in a positive way and inspire you to step out of your comfort zone?

BE RECONCILED TO YOURSELF

The topic of dissatisfaction always reminds me of a cow in a lovely green meadow, kneeling down on its front legs next to the fence, its neck craned uncomfortably, and its tongue stretched as far as possible to reach that one perfect piece of grass just on the other side in the neighbour's meadow. Behind the cow, just under its own tail, is a patch of a few dozen examples of the same kind of grass, but the grass always seems greener on the other side.

We often act in the same way. God has given each person a particular amount of land to conquer and possess. He has given each of us particular talents and a specific area of influence. But often, we stretch and strain ourselves to get something that was never meant for us and isn't good for us. We need to possess the New Land that God intends for us.

The talented American pianist Keith Jarrett was in Cologne, Germany on 24 January 1975 for an improvisational solo concert.[22] The idea was for him to create impromptu music out of nothing. Unfortunately, almost everything that could have gone wrong in advance of the performance did go wrong. Jarrett didn't sleep much the night before because he had to get up early to drive from Switzerland to Cologne. When he arrived at the concert hall, there was an unwelcome surprise awaiting him. Instead of the Bösendorfer 290 Imperial concert grand piano (the Rolls-Royce of concert instruments) that had been ordered, there was only a mediocre upright grand that would only have been used for rehearsals. But that wasn't the only bad news: the piano was also out of tune, the pedals didn't work, and some of the keys stuck. On top of all that, the catered pre-concert dinner was delivered far too late for Jarrett to eat before the performance. Nobody would have blamed him for simply cancelling the sold-out concert with its 1,400 audience members. But people convinced him to go on anyway. At first, they also wanted to cancel the planned live recording of the evening; however, they decided to record it anyway, as a kind of equipment test. Keith Jarrett sat down at the piano and began to play, despite all the challenges he faced. He simply played on the areas of the piano that more or less worked properly. The result was not just a run-of-the-mill piano concert, but rather an above-average, exuberant, overwhelming success that sold some 3.5 million CDs and record albums, becoming the best-selling jazz solo album and the highest selling piano solo album in the world; an astounding piece of music that never would have existed or been heard if Keith Jarrett had refused to accept the situation given to him and hadn't tried to make the best of it – just as Jesus took a couple of fish and a few pieces of bread when he saw thousands of hungry people in front of him (Matthew 14:13–21).

The bottom line is simple: take whatever God has entrusted to you and use it. Don't complain because your life's piano isn't a concert grand, as you would have liked, or that a couple of keys are stuck or even missing; just play the best song that you can in your situation. Take and use what God has placed before you and don't miss out on divine opportunities just because you are struggling with the way your life has turned out. There are always things that could be better, and there will always be things that are not exactly as you would have liked them to be. But it is not worth spending your entire life hiding behind the limitations and imperfections in your story. We all have to reconcile ourselves to these things – to accept who we are and what has made us this way. Embrace the circumstances of your life, embrace your mediocre grand piano. This is what Jesus meant when he said that each person should take up his or her cross daily (Matthew 16:24). Only those who take up their cross can also wear the crown.

I meet lots of people who never step into New Land because some particular factor in life isn't quite right. They are waiting until their finances are better, until they find the right partner, until their calling has been clarified, or until they are in a better situation to move house; or they refuse to go at all because they have a horrible past, because they have failed miserably in certain situations, or because they don't come from an ideal family background. They put themselves into a "temporary phase" and communicate it that way, too. It makes me wince to see that these phases often last for decades without an end in sight.

The truth is that often we simply lack the courage to seize the things God has put before us. No, the circumstances are not perfect, and yes, there are many other people who are better suited for the job, but we also have to recognize that God supports us in these situations. "Yes," he says, "I have chosen you especially for this situation, for this moment." And his "yes" is more trustworthy than all our concerns and fears. Take a seat at the piano and try to forget your weariness, your hunger, and your cluelessness; just play the best music of your life. And even if two-thirds of the keys are stuck, you can still make beautiful music on the other ones.

The question is not how good you are at something or whether the situation is optimal, but rather, whether you will stop searching for that unattainable grand piano and instead begin to play the music that God has placed on the music stand in front of you. Remember: you are supposed to play God's piece; you don't have to do everything that comes your way. You don't have to say "yes" and "amen" to everything all the time. It is important to know the difference between these two things.

What has God placed before you right now?

Why are you refusing to play your song?

It is completely OK to admit to God that you are afraid of what he has set before you. He likes when we share honestly with him what we want, as long as we remain open for what he wants for us. When I was about eighteen years old, a number of signs came together in the course of a few weeks to show me that God probably wanted me to become a preacher. In a state of panic, I vehemently and repeatedly prayed, "Dear God, if you want me to preach, then please give me a clear 'yes'. But please say 'no'."

Seldom have I prayed more urgently or passionately, and it was still a very unsuccessful prayer. You could call it an "anti-answer", since I have now been preaching for more than half my life. Today, there is nothing I would rather do. There are few things that fulfil me in the same way as preaching. God knows us much better than we know ourselves. He knows the areas of our hearts that remain hidden or unexplored. He has not only read the user manual of our hearts, he actually wrote it and put all the parts together. He knows exactly what is in your heart, perhaps slumbering and hidden at the moment, and he knows what areas of New Land still need to be discovered. "The boundary lines have fallen for me in pleasant places; surely I have a delightful inheritance" (Psalm 16:6, NIV). It is essential that we reconcile ourselves to our land – the inheritance we have received from God. A Newlandic spirit means accepting our circumstances and still being willing to take decisive, powerful steps into the future.

Trust what he puts in front of you. Play your own piano.

REMAIN A LEARNER

There are things to be learned in all phases of life, and we should remain learners throughout. That was God's original idea for people, and, although we are part of the fallen creation, his intention for us to keep learning remains intact into eternity. Readiness to learn is, therefore, a fundamental quality of a Newlandic spirit.

We must keep on learning because we will never have everything under control in life, and we will never be complete as individuals. God reveals himself to us only partially. Our understanding of our own identity is always fragmented, and much of what we can see before us is still at least partially hidden from view.

In life, we are always challenged to think in new ways, to learn new things, and to accept paradigm shifts. This might sound incredibly exhausting to you: "Can't we just leave things the way they are?" Well, sure. It can even become damaging if you constantly have your foot on the accelerator, giving everything you've got. Always giving 100 per cent is not a good thing – something that you will certainly realize if you ever try to donate blood.

Walking the path of discipleship is as normal as the rotation of the earth and is certainly not exhausting. Rotation gives us a pleasant rhythm of day and night and allows us to live and move around normally on the earth's surface. If you stand on the equator, you will have travelled more than 40,000 km in one day at a speed of 1,670 km/h, but you feel fine and no exertion is required. But that's not all. Our planet is travelling at a median speed of 29.78 km/second around the Sun: that is about 107,000 km/h. Then there is the entire solar system, which moves at a speed of 280 km/second around the Milky Way. That is about one million km/h.[23] Our motorway speed limits seem ridiculous in comparison. But if the earth stopped, inertia would cause everything that wasn't firmly fixed in place – that includes you and me – to jolt to the east at a speed of 1,670 km/h. Devastating natural disasters from hurricanes to earthquakes and floods would be the result, and temperatures would be completely thrown off balance. The fact is, nobody would suggest that the earth should take a break from rotating. And just like the earth, we need the steady movement of discipleship to help our faith remain in balance. But it doesn't take much effort to keep moving.

I was surprised to find out that constant learning and internal growth are a natural part of life from the beginning to now and into eternity. This dramatically increases my joyful anticipation of heaven. The usual idea that we will be singing songs of praise up there, accompanied by a heavenly symphony of harps for all eternity, sends a cold chill down my spine. It's no wonder that most people don't want to go there right now, even though they hope to end up there one day. We need to realize that the focus of our future life probably won't be that different from the here and now because God will return everything to his originally intended plan when he makes the New Heaven and the New Earth. This fills me with euphoric expectation. Eternity will be a huge upgrade from our current lives; as if you had booked a standing-room-only spot on the plane and then find yourself sitting in a massage chair in business class.

But even in heaven, we will not have finished learning. Indeed, we will continue to become more like Christ, but in heaven I will still be me and not just a clone of Christ. Perhaps this makes you think of John's statement that our journey to become like Christ will be complete when we enter heaven.

> *"Beloved, we are God's children right now; however, it is not yet apparent what we will become. But we do know that when it is finally made visible, we will be just like him, for we will see him as he truly is."*
> (1 John 3:2, TPT)

Although we will be like Christ, we will not become Christ himself. God continues to speak of his "children" and not about "clones". Being like him does not mean that we will be exactly like God with all his power and wisdom, but that we will become like him in that we will share certain abilities and characteristics. This is why the final phrase in that verse "for we will see him as he truly is" is so important to understand. We will be like him because we will see things as he sees them – namely, as they truly are. And we will be like him because we will also be without sin, but we will still not be all-knowing. Instead, we will stand in the presence of the omniscient one. We will not BE God; we will be WITH God. He is the only thing in the universe that does not change (Hebrews 13:8, James 1:17, NIV).

Heaven and the future earth will bring us on an amazing voyage of discovery for all eternity. We will continue to encounter new and exciting aspects of God and his New Land. Isn't that exciting? Perhaps you can still vaguely remember learning about prime numbers in your maths class at school. These are numbers larger than one that are only divisible by themselves or one. In the fourth century BC, the Greek mathematician Euclid discovered that every generation would have its own largest prime number. This is because in an endless list, there can never be one that is the absolute largest. Each generation will just keep adding to the list.

The largest prime number to date was discovered on 7 January 2016: $2^{74,207,281}-1$. That's a number with 22,338,618 decimal digits. It will not be the largest one for long, because future computers will provide better possibilities to discover more prime numbers. But none of those will ever be the last one, because there will always be another "largest" prime number. That is exactly how God designed our lives. He has planted godly qualities inside us, and we will never be finished discovering them.

If prime numbers don't give you an endorphin rush, then replace that with all the "good works" (Ephesians 2:10) that God has prepared for you to do in the future. There is no reason to think that these works will be limited to our earthly lifetimes. There are enough good works awaiting you to last into eternity. Ultimately, we will receive an imperishable and flawless inheritance (1 Peter 1:4), and that will certainly include something to do. Every time you uncover one of those works, you can be sure that another will follow and that there will always be a new "last one" for you to find. At some point, God will complete your process of becoming like Christ, but your personal voyage of discovery and the adventure you call life will continue.

Peter often writes about knowing God more and more, for example in 2 Peter 1:2: "I pray that God will be kind to you and will let you live in perfect peace! May you keep learning more and more about God and our Lord Jesus" (CEV).

The fact that we will spend eternity learning and discovering reveals what God intends for us, but it also awakens a sense of joyful anticipation for an age that will be anything but an endless, boring status quo. That is why it is so important for me to show that a basic curiosity and interest in discovering God and ourselves in new ways has been planted in our hearts by God. We inherently desire to know more about God, ourselves, the people around us, our marriages, and to develop new interests and abilities. Learning is a part of the Newlandic experience. It changes the way we interact with one another, how we live out our faith, how we develop, and how we encourage people to become excited about the future. When people apply for a job with Campus für Christus, one of my central requirements is that they are prepared to learn new things. If someone isn't interested in learning, then problems are destined to happen, regardless of their professional competence.

Jesus himself prescribed ongoing learning when he challenged those around him to "Learn from me" (Matthew 11:29). In Matthew 9:13 and 12:7, Jesus sends people out to learn and reflect on things he has shared.

In addition to the need to be reconciled to our own life story, readiness to learn is another fundamental trait of a Newlandic spirit. It permeates our being and affects the way we conduct our relationships and how we engage with people. Those who are ready to learn have a much higher tolerance for people who think differently from them, for the simple fact that they are convinced that an encounter with such a person is an opportunity to learn something new. We can acquire this trait by learning to courageously ask questions if we don't understand something, by listening instead of immediately trying to convince the other person of our way of thinking, and by being on the lookout for new things that will challenge us. Often, life's true treasures are buried a bit.

From whom have you recently learned something new? Do you enjoy learning, or is it generally something you find difficult? What was learning like for you earlier in life, back at school?

FOCUS ON THE RIGHT THING

Since 1211, the city of London has been paying rent to the royal household for two areas of land.[24] The rental fee is: one knife, one axe, six oversized horseshoes, and sixty-one nails. I have no idea what use the Queen has for all the axes she has received over the past few decades! And the best part is that no one knows exactly where the two parcels of land are located. The contract is clear and absolutely correct – but it no longer makes any sense. It is the same with religious exercises or traditions that we adopt and continue to practise without understanding where they have come from or without considering whether or not they remain valid or need to be adapted in some way. Being correct doesn't always mean you are right. I'm not calling people to revolt or suggesting that we should begin sneakily circumventing existing rules – although sometimes that can produce good results. Take, for example, the story of Cistercian lay monk Brother Jacob from the town of Maulbronn in Germany. During the famine of the Thirty Years' War in the seventeenth century, Brother Jacob miraculously received a piece of meat. However, because it was during Lent and he was abstaining from meat, he knew he wasn't allowed to eat it. He couldn't bring himself to throw it away, so he chopped it up into little pieces, mixed it with some spinach and herbs, and hid the mixture inside some dough so that he could eat it himself.

Somewhere along the way, these "Maulbronner Nudeltaschen" (or "Maulbronn dumplings") he had invented became known as "Maultaschen", which the cheeky monk called "The Good Lord's Little Cheat Treats".

The call to break away from correctness is not about speaking out of a rebellious attitude; I'm not interested in creating a group of wise guys. Rather, my plea is that we do not miss opportunities to do God's will out of a sheer desire for correctness, because his will can sometimes appear to be the exact opposite of what our religious system dictates. If we want to discover New Land, then we need to learn to obey God more than people (Acts 5:29) and we cannot allow ourselves to make fulfilling expectations our highest priority.

In his book *The Gaze of Mercy: A Commentary on Divine and Human Mercy*, Raniero Cantalamessa shares a new interpretation of the parable of the Good Samaritan (Luke 10), giving that familiar story a new twist.[25] A badly beaten man is lying half-dead in a ditch by the side of the road and two pious men, a priest and a Levite, walk right by him. Every time I read the details of how those "hypocrites" fail to care for the hurt man, a sense of outrage starts to grow in my heart. But Cantalamessa describes that both men were acting according to their religious guidelines – the Mosaic Law – and they did exactly what they were supposed to do. Because they had to assume that the man was already dead, they were forbidden to approach him and were not allowed to touch his body. Had they done so, they would have made themselves unclean and would not have been able to carry out their religious duties (Leviticus 21:1). As a result, we can say that they acted quite appropriately in walking past the man without touching him. Nevertheless, Jesus says we should behave like the Samaritan, who took care of the man out of love for his neighbour. So, you should not just stick to the Law, no matter how good and necessary it may be.[26] Being correct doesn't always mean that you are right, and doing the correct thing doesn't automatically mean you have done what is right, although Jesus was certainly correct. He didn't simply set himself above the Law; instead, he fulfilled it in his love and, at the same time, placed it within a larger frame of reference.

Sometimes we get the impression that Jesus just brushed the Law under the carpet; for example, when he healed people on the sabbath. But that is not the case. The confrontations Jesus had with them were based more on the fact that the rabbis had created a complex network of rules and regulations around the original Law (that is, by defining exact, specific cases in which performing a healing on the sabbath was permissible: in the case of acute life endangerment, the use of medicinal remedies was permitted, including those that would have been prepared using a mortar and pestle). Additionally, the various rabbis and rabbinical schools often took up opposing positions around a specific issue; they were seldom united in their opinions. Jesus had a problem with all this added "small print". Faith has little to do with keeping a strict set of religious regulations. That is why Jesus called their attention to the true meaning and purpose of the sabbath. "Then Jesus asked, 'On the Sabbath should we do good deeds or evil deeds? Should we save someone's life or destroy it?'" (Luke 6:9, CEV). In asking that question, Jesus was referring to a well-known Jewish proverb of the day: "Whoever destroys a soul, it is considered as if he destroyed an entire world. And whoever saves a life, it is considered as if he saved an entire world" (Mishnah, Sanhedrin 4:5). With this reference, Jesus was saying that failing to help – even on the sabbath – is equal to destroying another person; a mistake, despite the fact that you have followed all the rules.

Jesus did things that upset many people, most of all the religious authorities. He spent time and shared a meal with the tax collector Zacchaeus, he had contact with lepers, and he hung out with dodgy characters. Lots of people thought he was wrong, but, in fact, it was exactly the right thing to do. More than anything else, Jesus wanted to do the right thing in God's eyes and, at the same time, to encourage people to join him by setting these goals for themselves. He wanted everyone to put love above everything else, because without it, even the most correct actions are worthless.

Legalism and a lack of love grow out of a piously correct type of faith without the aspect of discipleship. "Jesus said to those Jews who believed in him, 'When you continue to embrace all that I teach, you prove that you are my true followers. For if you embrace the truth, it will release more freedom into your lives'" (John 8:31–32, TPT). Discipleship – holding on to Jesus and his Word – leads us to truth and freedom and uncovers our false "spiritual correctness", which not only sucks the life out of us, but also kills all life around us. When people in your congregation constantly talk about what you can and cannot do, it slowly kills the faith of the people over time.

The fact that religious exercises are worthless without God's Spirit was something that the seven sons of a priest called Sceva had to learn the hard way (Acts 19:11–16, CEV). Because they had witnessed that people were healed by touching a cloth that had passed over Paul's hair, they tried to do the same thing in copy/paste fashion. They attempted to cast out demons with the words, "Come out in the name of that same Jesus that Paul preaches about!"

It's a nice idea, actually, and they had experienced that the Paul–Jesus combo was very powerful. They expected the demons to be so impressed and terrified that they would leave immediately. But they had a problem, because they were only using a religious formula – they didn't know Jesus themselves or have any identity in Christ. That is why the evil spirit responded to them by saying, "I know Jesus! And I have heard about Paul. But who are you?" Then the evil spirit attacked the brothers and beat them until their clothes hung in rags and they were forced to run home naked and bleeding.

I'm glad that I know exactly who I am in Christ, because I no longer live, but he lives in me. I never want to be somewhere preaching about Jesus, casually throwing in some pious stories from the New Testament for good measure, only to be interrupted by a screeching voice from above that says, "I know Jesus. I met Paul a couple of centuries ago. But who are you?" I'll spare you – and myself – the rest of the details.

Those seven sons of Sceva said all the right things by reciting their special formula to cast out demons. On some level they were correct. But it was still not exactly right; it remained only a religious exercise.

Living with a Newlandic spirit doesn't mean you always have to get everything right, but that you should always try to do what is right in God's eyes. This challenges us to walk closely with Jesus, to listen to the voice of the Holy Spirit, and to follow what he tells us to do. You will probably have to dare to do new things and think new things. "What would life be if we hadn't courage to attempt anything?" asked Vincent van Gogh. And if you do not behave according to the expected standards, this can quickly cause irritation in your environment (family, workplace, church, and so on).

Where are you at risk of getting caught up in "spiritual correctness" instead of doing the right thing in God's eyes?

A Newlandic spirit searches passionately for what is right, not what is correct. While correctness leads to dead religion, doing the right thing leads to a living faith. God isn't looking for legal correctness or self-infatuated rebels. He is looking for people who are willing to do the right thing by dedicating themselves to godly love and by listening to the voice of the Holy Spirit every day.

CROSS THE DESERT

It usually takes more than a click of your fingers before going to bed to ensure you'll wake up the next morning in New Land. The Israelites had their own desert experience before they entered the Promised Land. Think about the supernatural provision they experienced and the ways God led them during that time. Those priceless experiences had to have made a deep and lasting impression on them – even if they often forgot things quite quickly. We often want to enter that wonderful New Land, but we would prefer to do it without all the hardships along the way. We want Paul's unshakeable faith, but we forget that it only grew strong due to his time in prison, torture, whippings, a shipwreck, and lots of other unpleasant experiences. We want the miracles without the persecution, endless trust in God without suffering, and sanctification without being sharpened by others. There is a lot of desert to cross before you get to the Promised Land.

If you want to enter New Land you have to put up with hot sand under your feet. And that's not that easy. Sometimes the desert surrounds you before you have even seen New Land on the horizon, and it hits you with the full force of its merciless heat and perilous conditions. It's unexpected and unbelievably harsh. You lose your job. You experience an unplanned pregnancy, or you find out that you will never be able to have children at all. Someone else gets the apprenticeship spot you were counting on or you fail an important exam. It's the words "I don't love you anymore" slapping you in the face, or the confession "I had an affair". Maybe news like "I have cancer" or "Your sister was killed in an accident this morning". It only takes a second and you are standing barefoot on hot sand, the horizon glimmering in the scorching heat, and you don't know where your life is going, or whether you can keep going at all. The smell of emptiness and death hang mercilessly in the air as dark clouds begin to rumble ominously overhead.

Desert times can be unbearable and seem an unending monotony. The Israelites ate manna day in, day out, just like we had rice three times a day in the Philippines. Sometimes we ate dry toast instead, just to be able to escape the rice and to give ourselves the illusion of a more balanced diet.

It is important to go through life with the hope that the New Land that God has prepared for you is actually out there. But we cannot shorten or skip over the desert times completely; instead, we can learn to accept those difficult parts of the journey and hold on tightly to God in those times. Or, as David so aptly put it, "Show me your ways, Lord, teach me your paths. Guide me in your truth and teach me, for you are God my Saviour, and my hope is in you all day long" (Psalm 25:4–5, NIV).

We tend to make prayer one-sided by trying to use it to keep all unpleasant things at bay. We want to be transported from the desert directly to the oasis. But there are things that can only be learned in the desert. And it seems that these steps of learning are the same steps that help us move out of the desert.

In 1896, Germany introduced the important rule that a football pitch must be free of trees and shrubs. In fact, for some games today, I wish there were still a few trees dotted around the pitch, because it would give the game a healthy, uncontrollable component and prevent it from always being so strategic and planned. Unfortunately in life, the "treeless zone" rule has never been introduced. So it may well be that a ball unexpectedly changes direction or we run painfully into a tree trunk.

There are times in life when everything runs smoothly; at other times, obstacles stand in our way. David also experienced similar ups and downs. He was ignored by his father and not even called in when a king was to be selected from the members of his family. In the end, though, he is the one who is crowned. As a shepherd, he was not spared the terror of lion and bear attacks. He became a hero when he defeated Goliath, but then he had to run for his life from Saul. One time, he even hid with his men in a cave: "Saul went into the cave to relieve himself. David and his men were hiding at the back of the cave" (1 Samuel 24:3, CEV).

I couldn't get my head around this situation when I tried to imagine it. Think about it: you are running away from Saul, you hide yourself somewhere in a cave, and then your pursuer comes into that very cave and defecates right under your nose. It doesn't get any worse than that. Of course, things could have ended badly for Saul, too, if David had not acted according to God's rules and spared him in that situation. Otherwise, Saul's demise would have gone down in history with the inglorious cause of death listed as defecation.

David spared Saul many times, although Saul wanted to kill him. David understood that he would not be blessed if he took hold of the throne for himself. Instead, he left it up to God to determine the timing of Saul's end – as well as the end of his own desert period. We would do well to follow that example and not to take things for ourselves that are not yet meant for us. Those things will never receive God's blessing. That is why we sometimes have to follow the unpleasant path to the end, even when there seems to be a viable shortcut.

Have you ever realized that we often read the Bible with the assumption that God will intervene to replace a rocky path with a perfectly straight road? In reality, many of our heroes of faith have had to walk through fire on their journeys – literally for Daniel's friends (Daniel 3). Just pick someone; Noah, for example. Yes, he and his family were rescued from the flood, but forty days in a rocking ark filled with a challenging mix of zoo-like scents and smells would probably not qualify as a dream cruise. Prayer alone will not save us from every lions' den, furnace, or crash with a tree trunk – but at least it will help us get through these trials. The result is that we end up in a completely different place afterwards: in New Land. Even if people put obstacles in our path, it will all work together for our good in the end, as Romans 8:28 promises. Or as Johann Wolfgang von Goethe, the famous German poet, put it, "You can also build something beautiful out of the stones that have been placed in your path." Aristotle phrased it in this way: "We cannot change the wind, but we can set the sails right."

There is a type of coffee bean that is a lot more savvy than us people, because it has figured out that unpleasant processes are sometimes necessary in order to reach a desired destination.

We discovered the famous Kape Musang, wild cat coffee, in the Philippines. It is produced from happy, free-range coffee beans. However, the beans are not simply harvested by people; instead, they experience an unpleasant fate, namely, being eaten by wild cats. Each lowly coffee bean has to go through a trial, by literally going through a wild cat. The wild cats' excrement is collected and the beans are "harvested". The world's best coffee is made from these beans.

Life feels just like this process at times. You have to go through suffering, and when you come out the other side, you have been humbled by the experience. As with those beans, at the end of the process, when everything has been stripped away, you feel worthless. You frequently ask "Why me?" when you are lying flat on the ground. It would be sad, indeed, if there wasn't a surprising twist to the story: the finishing touch that makes all the difference.

People discovered that as the coffee beans pass through a wild cat's stomach, they undergo a unique chemical process that creates a delicious aroma in the coffee. This rare offering has its price; in Europe, the coffee is sold at about 1,000 Euro per kilo – the most expensive coffee in the world. Things can get pretty uncomfortable in life sometimes. But, in the right hands – in God's hands – your life is highly valued, priceless. He uses things that others disregard or ignore and makes the best out of your life. If you are lying in the dirt right now, allow God to lift you up and put you through a process. He will make something wonderful out of you!

Maybe you have given up somewhere along the way because it all just seems too much to handle. But if you're considering giving up, it's only fair to take a moment and think back to why you started in the first place. And why you've hung on until now.

What desert times have you experienced in your life? What New Land have you discovered as a result of those times?

CHASING THE INVISIBLE

In 2 Kings 6 we read about the battle between the Arameans and the Israelites. The king of Aram was quite peeved when the prophet Elisha shared the battle plans with his enemy, the Israelite king. When he heard that Elisha was in Dothan, he sent a huge army out to surround the prophet in an overnight military operation.

> *When the servant of the man of God got up and went out early the next morning, an army with horses and chariots had surrounded the city. 'Oh no, my lord! What shall we do?' the servant asked.*
>
> (2 Kings 6:15, NIV)

I can imagine that servant waking up with a deep yawn, stretching his arms, and walking outside, only to be startled as he looked through sleep-filled eyes at the huge army that had surrounded their city. All six litres of his blood would have gone directly to his feet in seconds; he probably had to fight the urge to be sick or even faint as he turned and dashed to Elisha. When I saw the sea of slobbering orcs encamped in front of the city in the film *Lord of the Rings: The Return of the King*, I had a similar feeling. And I was not even in that city, I was just sitting on the sofa with a bag of crisps. Elisha, however, was tough (verses 16–17):

'Don't be afraid,' the prophet answered. 'Those who are with us are more than those who are with them.' And Elisha prayed, 'Open his eyes, Lord, so that he may see.' Then the Lord opened the servant's eyes, and he looked and saw the hills full of horses and chariots of fire all around Elisha.

Unbelievable! And what an utterly different perspective. While the servant only saw what his eyes showed him – actually very normal and understandable – Elisha perceived the bigger picture, the invisible reality. He had an eye for a greater reality. This perspective is unbelievably helpful in life.

We need to learn to perceive the invisible. To look at people and see not only what is visible with the naked eye, but what God has put inside them as well. To not only realize how bad a situation is, but also see opportunities for God to be glorified through those difficulties. To see not only what is, but also what could be. When we begin to see things through Newlandic eyes, we see life with a new hue. "Things that are seen don't last forever, but things that are not seen are eternal. That's why we keep our minds on the things that cannot be seen" (2 Corinthians 4:18, CEV).

In my mind, learning to see the invisible is one of the most important abilities for someone who leads others (from house husband to pastor to employer). We can only go before people if we are able to see what God has prepared for us, and if we are willing to courageously step into it by faith. We need to learn to sense how God wants to use situations and circumstances. Faith is being able to see what is not yet visible, and having a Newlandic spirit is about being on the lookout for it in daily life. Anyone who denies the invisible is like a pilot who can only fly by sight. Faith means not only living out of our own experience, but walking in the promises of God as well.

Experiences often fool us, appearing to be the true reality, but they may lead us down a completely wrong path. I was once in a friend's car driving through the mountains. As we were passing through a village with very narrow streets, he took a blind bend past a house without stopping to look for oncoming traffic. In the passenger seat, I automatically jumped on my pseudo-brakes and asked, with more than a hint of irritation, what he would have done if another car had been coming toward us! His answer was quite pragmatic: "I've driven through here lots of times, and I've never passed another car." But basing your actions on your experiences alone can be tricky. Of course, they are important, in faith as well, because they help us put down roots. But if you rely solely on your own experiences, your tree of faith will die out as soon as you hit a dry spell without new experiences.

Much of what God has prepared for us in the future has already been written somewhere, although it is not yet visible to us. It's as if God has used one of those invisible ink pens that I loved so much as a kid. In the right light, for example under a UV lamp, the words suddenly become visible. Jesus himself is the perfect light for viewing things (John 8:12). If I can learn to look at situations in my life through his eyes, then I can get a glimpse of the things that are not yet readily visible.

In Hebrews 11:27 (CEV) we read, "Because of his faith, Moses left Egypt. Moses had seen the invisible God and wasn't afraid of the king's anger." And this brings us to another fundamental aspect of faith. "Faith makes us sure of what we hope for and gives us proof of what we cannot see" (Hebrews 11:1, CEV).

Promises are some of the unseen things strewn across the path of our lives. If we want to see the invisible, the promises are a part of the deal, or perhaps you could say clinging to the promises. God loves this kind of tenacity.

"We wish that each of you would always be eager to show how strong and lasting your hope really is. Then you would never be lazy. You would be following the example of those who had faith and were patient until God kept his promise to them" (Hebrews 6:11–12, CEV). This encouragement is worth its weight in gold. I am convinced that the reason we don't always reach our full potential in life is because we have stopped chasing after God's promises. If you keep hunting for divine promises like you hunt those Pokémon GO characters, you will certainly receive them.

I have had to cling to God's promises time and time again throughout my life, and I haven't been disappointed. When I was a teenager, I started to have dreams of standing in a stadium. At some point, I realized that this dream was from God, something he had planted in my heart, not something that my own pride had created. I held on tightly to that promise in my heart. Once I applied to be the speaker at a large event, and I had to learn the hard way that we don't need to help God to fulfil his promises. I just had to trust in his timing. About twenty years later, I spoke in a stadium for the first time. It was one of the most powerful experiences of my life, not because of the stadium, but because I was able to experience God's faithfulness to fulfil his promises when we wait faithfully on him.

God's perspective is so much broader than ours, and he doesn't seem to get stressed out at all – like we tend to do. When I was part of a new church plant, we decided to rent an old factory building, a former weaving plant. We wanted to see whether God had something planned for that place and for us. About two months later, we got our answer in an impressive way. We heard about a man who had worked in that factory years ago and had heard from God some twenty-five years earlier that he should pray for it, because God planned to make it a place for young people to meet in his name. We started our church in exactly that place about twenty-five years after the man had received God's promise, and many people came to faith in that place. If you cling to God's promises, he will not disappoint you.

When I was putting my kids to bed recently, we read the Abraham story. I was moved by the strength of his faith and his faithfulness. God challenged him to head for New Land. He had more or less the same reaction I would have to those instructions: he wanted to know where he was going. But God just assured him that he would show him along the way (Hebrews 11:8 and Genesis 12:1). I would probably just sit down in protest – and out of fear – while Abraham and his whole family packed all their belongings and headed out for parts unknown.

> *Faith motivated Abraham to obey God's call and leave the familiar to discover the territory he was destined to inherit from God. So he left with only a promise and without even knowing ahead of time where he was going, Abraham stepped out in faith.*
> (Hebrews 11:8, TPT)

Eventually, he actually arrived in his beautiful Promised Land – but he still felt like a stranger in a foreign country, and so it remained (Hebrews 11:9). That's how it can be for us, too. Walking with God isn't always sunny skies and smooth sailing. Sometimes we won't feel quite at home, although we are in exactly the place God wants us to be. Abraham receives the promise that an entire people will come from him, despite the fact that both he and his wife are very old and have no children. Just one more thing that he cannot see. So it seems logical that even Abraham started to have doubts. Many biblical heroes of faith struggled with doubts at some point in their lives and lost sight of the invisible for a time. John the Baptist proclaimed nothing else but the coming Christ, and when Jesus arrived, even he had to ask, "Are you the one…?" (see Matthew 11:3).

These kinds of doubts are not wrong or unnecessary; rather, they support our growing faith. For example, if you continually irrigate grapevines, their roots will stay close to the surface and, when the next storm passes over, it will blow your vines all the way to Grape-Nirvana. Times of prolonged dryness force the roots to go deep. It works the same with our faith – times of drought and doubt force our roots to go deep in search of God's heart.

I love the point in the story where God challenges doubting Abraham to come out of his tent (Genesis 15:5). God shows him the starry night sky and promises to give him descendants as numerous as the stars. Could it be that we also hide ourselves in a stuffy little tent in terms of our faith? We see only the wall of the tent in front of us, the beautiful moonlight makes it look a sickly green, and instead of the fresh smell of the outdoors, we only smell the musty odour of a well-used sleeping bag and stinky hiking socks. God needs to call out to us all, saying, "Come out of the tent!" If we heed his call, we will be treated to an unbelievably breathtaking scene, the greater dimension of the unseen world.

Abraham clung to that promise and changed his point of view. He looked up to heaven instead of at the wall of his tent.

Another person who learned to cling on was Abraham's grandson Jacob. I am fascinated by the fact that, unlike his brother Esau, Jacob developed an eye for the invisible, a longing for God's blessing, and a readiness to do whatever it took to receive it. You can see that he inherited his grandfather's heart. Like Abraham, Jacob knew well that there is nothing better than receiving God's blessing and reaching out for the "not yet visible". But the blessing was tied to the birthright of the firstborn son, and that belonged to his brother Esau. However, Esau couldn't have cared less about the blessing that was rightfully his. One day, after a long and strenuous hunt, he came home hungry. Jacob had cooked a lentil stew, and Esau wanted some. Cunning Jacob offered him a portion in exchange for his birthright. The most shocking thing is that Esau agreed to the deal – a classic facepalm moment.

No matter how often I read that passage, the horror of it all gets me every time. Everything in me screams, "Stop! ESAU! Don't be stupid! Take the blessing! THE BLESSING!" But not only is Esau a good subject for morology – the study of nonsense – he must also be deaf. It is unbelievable what hunger can do to a man. I'm insufferable when I'm hungry. When I look at it from that perspective, it is easy to understand how Esau gave in. But what I really can't understand is the fact that he sold his birthright for lentils! Maybe for one of those deluxe burgers at a restaurant near me, or a juicy sirloin steak from the grill, but certainly not lentils!

The point is that we often act in exactly the same way. We lose sight of the big picture, of what we could have, or maybe of what we already had at some point in our lives, in order to satisfy our hunger. The problems of the here and now absorb us to the extent that we begin to fight our symptoms instead of considering the long-term consequences of our decisions; for example, I need a new employee, I need to change my living arrangements, I want to buy that now, or God has to answer this prayer.

What is your "lentil stew" that has made you let go of God's promise? What kind of "lentil soup" has made you sell your blessing and forfeit your New Land? What is making you feel hungry?

Don't let go of your promise, that thing you cannot see. Struggle with God like Jacob, who wrestled with an angel saying, "I will not let you go unless you bless me" (Genesis 32:26, NIV). God wants you to take your blessing more than anything else, so your participation in that plan is not optional. In Romans 9:13 (NIV) we read, "Jacob I loved, but Esau I hated." But why should God hate poor, hungry Esau, who had a moment of idiocy at the worst possible time, and love cunning Jacob, an obvious liar and cheat? Even the idea of divine predestination doesn't provide a wholly satisfactory answer to this question. The only thing that seems plausible is that God hated the fact that Esau chose lentils over the blessing in the first place. I don't think it is too extreme to say that God hates it when I turn down his blessing or that he hates it when I throw his blessings out the window and stop striving to see the big picture he wants to draw on the canvas of my life. Don't base your decisions on your hunger. That will only satisfy in the short term. Don't stop chasing after the unseen and unknown. Don't settle for a bowl of lentils when you can have a pot full of blessings.

10

STRA
TEG
IC

Conquering New Land

For Joshua, clinging to God's promise came with a great reward. God kept his promise: "The Lord promised to do many good things for Israel, and he kept his promise every time" (Joshua 21:45, CEV). In the book of Joshua, the Israelites have to conquer many cities and fight many battles on the way to possessing the land. And every city invasion and battle was different. We also have to conquer certain cities and to master different situations in our own lives – and each one requires a different strategy. When I have to sit an exam, I need to prepare well and then produce the desired result under pressure. I need a completely different strategy to overcome a bad habit or to keep my resolution to exercise more.

Take a moment, at the beginning of this chapter, to think of a situation in your life that is challenging you right now. Make a note of it and talk about it with God. Maybe one of Joshua's strategies will inspire you, or perhaps God has a completely new strategy in mind for your situation.

We will dive into some of these strategies now.

THE PATIENCE OF JERICHO

The Strategy: patience and trusting God (Joshua 6)

This was probably not one of Joshua's favourite city-conquering strategies: walking around the city in front of the enemy's arrows once daily for six days, then doing the same thing seven times on the seventh day. You could expect the defending armies to make a sally at some point, and then the Israelites wouldn't have had much of a chance to defend themselves, let alone make an attack, because they were spread out in a ring around the city. As an experienced warrior, Joshua probably had more promising battle tactics in his repertoire. But this was God's idea; probably not only to show the surrounding tribes, but also to prove to the Israelites themselves, that success comes from God alone.

One of my co-workers was once denied the opportunity to preach in a particular church based on the fact that he worked for Campus für Christus. I found the decision not only incomprehensible and unjust, but also incredibly rude. I kept wondering whether I should react in some way, whom I should write a letter to, and whether I should make the whole outrageous affair public. I wrote three emails to the responsible party, each one clearer than the last, and I deleted every one before pressing send. (In my heart of hearts, I knew when I wrote them that I would never actually send them. Still, it did my soul good to let out all my frustration over this injustice, a little bit like David did.) In the end, though, the Christ-like part of me wrestled the Old Boppi to the ground, and I started blessing that person for all I was worth.

Unfortunately, I don't overflow with wisdom and prudence as often as I'd like. In this particular situation, though, I kept blessing the person for months. After more than a year, I felt that I ought to call that leader and ask his advice about something, although it cost me a lot to approach that person. I did it, and all of a sudden, although we hadn't even been talking about the issue, he apologized for his earlier behaviour.

Not only had we cleared the air, but God turned everything around so that my former co-worker is now in a leadership role at that church and preaches there regularly. My logical, human reaction at the time would have caused a lot of damage. It is not always right to start a war and ride into a battle with all guns blazing. Sometimes it is better to wait, pray, and be patient. I am so glad that I chose this strategy for that battle and that I was able to makes laps of blessing around that city – until God brought the walls tumbling down.

When we encircle something or someone with prayer and blessing, we will often see walls begin to shake and fall. Perhaps there is a situation or a person in your life who needs the "Patience of Jericho" strategy? Start doing laps.

THE TRICK IN AI

The Strategy: be cunning (Joshua 7–8)

Joshua 7, which follows directly after the victory over Jericho, begins with the word "But" in many translations. You are never more vulnerable to suffering defeat than directly after a great victory. Success tends to make us careless. You don't think clearly in the wake of victory. Following Achan's disobedience in carrying off some of the spoils of war that had been dedicated wholly to God, the battle in Ai went very badly. Sometimes we think that the things we do are not really that bad, and, regardless of our devotion to the heavenly Father, we forget that we are dealing with a holy God.

The fact that the spies had completely underestimated the situation in Ai also contributed to the defeat. They talked about "a few men" in the city, saying that 2,000 to 3,000 Israelite troops would be enough for the battle. In reality, some 6,000 men lived in Ai. This led to Joshua's first painful defeat.

After Joshua solved the Achan problem with God's help, he was able to take the city of Ai successfully. This time, though, marching around in circles was not part of the plan. God told Joshua to conquer the city by tricking the people there. They lured the warriors out of the city and then took out the entire army.

When Jesus sent out his twelve apostles, he told them, "I am sending you out like sheep among wolves. Therefore be as shrewd as snakes and as innocent as doves" (Matthew 10:16, NIV). Although Jesus sends us as sheep, it doesn't mean that we are supposed to stand and look around us stupidly like sheep do. We find this slyness over and over again in the Bible. When the Israelites were oppressed by the Moabite king Eglon, God called Ehud as their deliverer. Ehud was left-handed, a seemingly unimportant detail we read in Judges 3:15, but a key component for the upcoming deliverance. Ehud made a 30 cm-long dagger, which he hid in a sheath on his right hip: perfectly placed for a left-handed person to draw quickly. This was probably why no one uncovered the plot when he came in to speak to King Eglon. He tricked the guards into leaving the room so that he was alone with the king, a stout man. Or, to be biblically accurate, "a very fat man" (Judges 3:17, CEV). Then he took the dagger in his left hand and stabbed Eglon in the stomach.

The Bible gives an unusually detailed account of what happened, describing how the dagger, including the handle, disappeared into the king's fat belly. As the servants stayed outside the door, waiting because they assumed the king was using the toilet, they missed the opportunity to save him and Ehud fled to safety. The Israelites defeated the Moabites, resulting in an eighty-year period of peace. I love the unvarnished images of this story. It was cunningly smart to choose a left-hander for such a mission.

There are many situations in everyday life when it is to our advantage to be cunning. It is not about deceiving people, acting on evil impulses, or keeping certain information from others in order to benefit in some way ourselves. Instead, being cunning refers to choosing our words wisely so as not to offend others as we move toward our goal.

Being cunning can also mean that God gives us creative ideas or a solution to a problem – maybe we should dare to do something completely unconventional or something that does not make any sense at first (of course, it will upon second glance).

Where could you use some of Joshua's cunning this week? Ask God for creative ideas and inspiration.

THE FLOW AT SHECHEM

The Strategy: look for what has been prepared for you (Joshua 8)

On the way to Mount Ebal and Mount Gerizim, Joshua led the people by Shechem. We don't read anything about the invasion of this city, which guards the opening of the valley between these two mountains, although it certainly would not have been possible just to walk past. Due to the lack of information, it is possible to deduce that the city simply gave up without a fight. It can also work like this in life – there are cities that you are able to conquer without a fight because God has already prepared everything. It just falls into your lap; these are the moments where everything works perfectly, flowing smoothly like water down a waterslide.

When I got the inspired idea to do a national campaign in Switzerland, we were already in the middle of preparations for our huge Explo Conference. It was obvious that we would not be able to raise funds for two large projects simultaneously, especially in light of the total amount needed; the national campaign alone was budgeted in the seven-digit range. So I promised God that I would give my all to make the project a success as long as he paid for it so that I didn't have to contact dozens of people to raise the money. The names of two businessmen came to mind, so I contacted them, and the idea for the campaign truly fell on perfectly prepared soil. Within just a few days, both men had pledged huge sums, enough for us to start the project with confidence. The result was not only an evangelistic campaign and the mobilization of many Christians throughout the country, but also increased unity and a stronger network among Christian leaders, the benefits of which we are still enjoying today.

Sometimes, though, things in life move forward haltingly, as if they were stuck in place. Then it is important to find out whether it is really the right thing to be doing at all. It could be that we are barking up the wrong tree, or perhaps it is just opposition that needs to be overcome. Both can feel confusingly similar.

At times, you have to get stuck into something – but if it is an uphill battle from A to Z, it is quite possible that it is not God's idea. Look for the prepared cities where initial opposition suddenly disappears. But it is not about always looking for the path of least resistance. Still, if you almost break down trying to do what you want to accomplish, if it eats up all your energy and you cannot move forward, there is a good chance that you are not on the path that God has planned for you. If God is in it, it will become easy at some point (Matthew 11:30).

THE AMORITE MIRACLE

The Strategy: a supernatural solution (Joshua 10)

Joshua attacked the united army of the five Amorite kings in an open field. Even the journey to the battlefield was arduous and tiring – the Israelites had to march 40 km in the dark across nearly impassable, mountainous terrain. This fact alone shows that Joshua was counting on God's intervention, since a victory in battle after the strain of such a march was anything but realistic. That victory was not won by encircling the enemy or through cunning tricks, and nothing felt like it was flowing smoothly after such a long journey. God intervened in a supernatural way: he sent stones to rain down on the Amorites, killing more than any attack by Joshua's army would ever have managed. Joshua also caused the Sun to stand still, although I'm not sure quite how he did it (Joshua 10:13). In the end, the victory was an interplay of human effort and an even greater portion of the supernatural.

David Ben-Gurion, the first Prime Minister of Israel, said, "In order to be a realist, you must believe in miracles." It is always good to be on the lookout for the supernatural work of God. His miracles are still a reality today; he continues to add new chapters to the book of Acts. We hear so many stories of God's supernatural activity, especially in places where the persecution of Christians and minorities is most severe. People are coming to faith through dreams or experiencing God's intervention in unbelievable ways. At a leaders' meeting of the underground church in Cairo, a young Egyptian man shared a dream he had had. He told the group how Jesus had shown him a specific address and directed him to go there and tell the people in that house about him. The man mustered all his courage and knocked on the door of the house Jesus had shown him. To his surprise, an imam opened the door. Should he really tell him about God? He trusted God and said, "Jesus has sent me to tell you about him."

The man was even more surprised when the imam raised his hands and said, "Hallelujah," pulling him into the living room. Twelve other imams were sitting in a circle and one of them explained, "We all came to faith in Jesus Christ a few weeks ago through a Christian television programme. We started reading the Bible, but we don't understand everything. We've been praying that God would send someone to explain his Word to us. Now you're finally here. Where have you been?"

This is just one miracle among many that God is doing in regions around the world that have been shaken by crisis. At the same time, special moments are also happening closer to home, when heaven touches earth to heal people, transform hearts, and bring change to impossible situations.

But the tension remains because not all people receive healing, although others have prayed for them. Healing is a component of the new kingdom that awaits us. We still live in the fallen creation. Right now, we have no explicit right to healing and no claim that God has to give us all his blessings here on earth. But every so often, the glory of God's new kingdom, which has already started here and now, flows down to earth and undeserved supernatural things occur – like drops of mercy from heaven. God longs for us to yearn for a relationship with him, too, and for us to reach out to find miracles of all kinds. Still, we should remember not to become infatuated with the miracles, but with the one who works them. But we Christians could use a bit more courage in order to believe in the reality of the supernatural and to act upon that belief. We can spread God's love unrestrained and extravagantly, pray for people, read the Bible together – even if a result is sometimes not immediately visible. You are responsible for praying, but not for the result. One significant element that contributes to revivals is people who step out and live lives that reflect personal awakening.

THE DEPENDENCY STRATEGY

We can learn a lot from Joshua about how to conquer New Land in the right way, even though our cities look different. Your life lies before you, with lots of promised New Land that God intends for you to enter. It is waiting to be conquered at the right time with the right strategy. Sometimes we come to a point where the view ahead is frightening, whether you are faced with an impassable river, an unconquerable city, or challenges that rear up like Anakim giants. Time and time again, God encourages Joshua and the Israelites by reminding them of the promise, "I've commanded you to be strong and brave. Don't ever be afraid or discouraged! I am the Lord your God, and I will be there to help you wherever you go" (Joshua 1:9, CEV). And God is also with you. Be courageous and do not fear.

God links his promises to requirements that are still valid for us today: "Any one of you can defeat a thousand enemy soldiers, because the Lord God fights for you, just as he promised. Be sure to always love the Lord your God" (Joshua 23:10–11, CEV).

Loving God is the best thing we can possibly do. And the most important. If I could give my children only one piece of advice in life, I would tell them that last verse: "Be sure to always love the Lord your God." When we focus on doing that, we will be able to walk into undeserved blessing over and over again, just like Joshua. "You didn't have to work for this land – I gave it to you. Now you live in towns you didn't build, and you eat grapes and olives from vineyards and trees you didn't plant" (Joshua 24:13, CEV).

The main point is that we cannot avoid needing to depend on God as we walk through life. We cannot simply use the same strategy for every situation and always expect success. In 1099, the Crusaders followed Joshua's example and began circling the walls of Jerusalem barefoot while fasting. Nothing came tumbling down, but at least they raised company morale and they ultimately conquered the city in another way.

Knowing how to trust God and act according to his mind in the various phases of our lives and at strategically important intersections is the overarching strategy – this is the background to all of Joshua's different strategies for success. When he trusted God fully, he experienced incredible victories.

Joshua's secret was listening to God's voice and following the path that God confirmed to him. That's how he was able to follow those divine plans with utter precision. "As the Lord commanded his servant Moses, so Moses commanded Joshua, and Joshua did it; he left nothing undone of all that the Lord commanded Moses" (Joshua 11:15, NIV). Joshua conquered the land piece by piece (Joshua 11:16), or at least the main centres throughout the country. God spoke to Joshua: "Now you are very old, but there is still a lot of land that Israel has not yet taken" (Joshua 13:1, CEV). It's the same in your life. No matter how much land you have already conquered, there will always be New Land that God intends for you to step into, because it will become a blessing for you and for those around you.

What is your strategy? In which areas of your life or daily activities do you typically ask God for advice? What do you do if you don't receive an answer?

Think about that little note I asked you to write down at the beginning of this chapter. We were thinking about a current situation that you need God's advice on. Bring it to God right now and write down the thoughts that go through your mind over the next four to five minutes. Does anything sound like God's voice to you? Can you make out a strategy yet?

There is one more important thought in closing. Sometimes Israel, under the leadership of Joshua, spared individuals and entire tribes, despite God's instructions to the contrary. That led to problems afterwards – as in the example of the fortress of Zion (Jerusalem) under the control of the Jebusites, which David had to conquer later (2 Samuel 5:7), as well as with the Anakim "giants" (Joshua 11). That's why David had to come face to face with Goliath (1 Samuel 17) – one of the descendants of the Anakim, who escaped to Gath. Disregarding God's commands leads entire societies into big problems.

It is worthwhile to fight the life battles that God has prepared for us and to do so thoroughly so that in the end, the following will have been said of your life: "Finally, there was peace in the land" (Joshua 11:23, CEV).

It is absolutely central that you conquer the New Land prepared for you together with God. Probably only a few of your life's battles will take on the epic proportions of those in the Bible. But at least some of them will have a huge impact on your life and the lives of many around you. Be brave and determined.

11

PRAGMATIC

Stepping into New Land

The first step to discovering New Land is to figure out where it awaits you. Then you have to dare to take a courageous step of faith to enter that new territory, and this is where things tend to fall apart. Now is a good time to take stock of things and see where you stand.

What part(s) of this book have spoken to you so far? Where do you see a need to examine or make changes in your life?

This chapter is about how you can move from standing on the border, looking longingly across into New Land, to taking practical steps to enter in and possess it. It can be helpful not to try to tackle too much at once, but to identify two or three concrete steps and plan exactly how you want to go about realizing them. It is also good to share your adventure plans with a couple of friends who will be able to support you along the way, and maybe even join you.

Or, perhaps you have got tired of the reading the term "Newlandic" again and again and you just can't hear it at all anymore. At the risk of trivializing everything else in this book, I would like to say that, ultimately, it's not about you and your new territory, but it's primarily about you and your Saviour. When you walk with him, you will automatically, and often surprisingly, find yourself in the middle of New Land. But sometimes you need to make a conscious decision about the direction you want to go in or what you want to work on.

During World War II, Hitler tried to boost the morale of his troops with the announcement of an amazing super-weapon.[27] Most of it remained just a collection of bizarre ideas scribbled on paper, but some things were actually implemented. One super-weapon that was fully developed was a new design for a high-pressure toilet for deep-sea submarines. The Type VII submarine was the backbone of the German navy in the Third Reich. They were 67 metres long and had capacity for a crew of sixty seamen. They could travel distances of up to 15,000 km. The U-1206 was one of the upgraded models fitted with the miracle toilet. Before that, all human waste produced by the fifty-man crew had to be stored within the sub until it was safe to dispose of it. To do so, they had to return to the surface, at the risk of being seen and fired upon by the enemy. With the new high-tech toilet, waste was directly transported outside the ship through a complex labyrinth of pipes and hoses and expelled into the ocean through a pressurized passage. It was so complicated that there was one specially trained crew member on board to operate all the valves in the right order during the disposal procedure.

The U-1206 set off on 6 April 1945 under the command of Captain-Lieutenant Karl-Adolf Schlitt. A week later, on 14 April, Schlitt felt the call of nature when they were somewhere along the Scottish coast. He trusted his instincts and experience in the use of toilets and, upon completion of the necessary business, he pulled the lever to flush. But it didn't work as planned. A forceful, stinking spray of water began to flood the sub. One survivor described how the submarine jolted and then began to sink "like a stone". In the middle of enemy territory, they were forced to surface, came under fire, and had to escape to land in rubber dinghies. Captain Schlitt had managed to sink his own submarine by using the toilet. It wouldn't surprise me if people had begun to use Captain Schlitt's name minus the c and the l.

What can we learn from this story? That it is important to pull the right levers. Our actions always have consequences, and in some cases it is not wise to do things yourself; you should call a specialist. It is never wrong to invite God to help you make complex decisions in your life instead of just moving ahead on your own until you're standing in front of a steaming pile of crap. In the end, there are a couple of specific levers that you can pull to move forward in this area.

DEMOLISH THE ROOF

There are so many "I ought to" sentences and an endless list of things I think about doing but give up on after only a short time. One of my legendary resolutions, "I think I'll fast this week and maybe keep going for forty days", ended miserably at lunch on the first day in a McDonald's restaurant. I still can't quite understand why Adam and Eve got tripped up by a piece of fruit. If it had been a burger tree, I wouldn't have any questions.

I ought to spend more time with my children, I ought to exercise more, I ought to pray more, bring my wife flowers more often, save more money, enjoy life more, be more thankful, give people more compliments, invest more time in the garden – but the only thing that I have from declaring all these resolutions is more failed attempts to improve myself, which just makes me more frustrated.

There are certainly things in life that we have to decide to do and then we have to stand up and do them. Sometimes it's just a matter of overcoming our own laziness, and it helps if we look for a couple of practical tricks to make things happen. For example, I wanted my first thoughts each morning to be about God and not about all the work I had to do that day, so I installed a "Verse of the Day" programme on my PC to help me focus on the right thing each morning.

In terms of tackling things, I'm a big fan of the attitude of those men who wanted to bring their paralysed friend to Jesus to be healed. At that time in his hometown region, Jesus was like Justin Bieber, Adele, and Roger Federer all rolled into one. Sometimes he even fled to a remote area to escape the crowds and the local paparazzi, although he wasn't always successful. When the people heard that he was staying in a house in Capernaum, he was inundated by the crowds. Everyone wanted to see Jesus and many hoped to be healed. Those four men carrying their paralysed friend couldn't get through. I probably would have just headed home and tried to find another opportunity to meet Jesus. But that's not what these four did. They climbed on top of the house and started demolishing the roof.

I would love to have seen the faces of the people in the house when they looked up to find the source of the bright light, the heat on their heads, and the light shower of dirt and dust raining down into their eyes. The four men lowered their friend down through the roof, leaving him directly at Jesus' feet, who forgave the man's sins and then healed him, too.

For me, the most surprising part is what motivated Jesus to act: "When Jesus saw how much faith they had…" (Mark 2:5, CEV). Of course, Jesus saw the heart and the faith of the paralysed man when he forgave his sins, but the thing that set it all in motion was the faith of those friends. Faith is not just a personal, individual thing; your faith makes a direct impact on the people around you – it sets things in motion.

How can you see faith? Perhaps it becomes clear when our passionate and pragmatic actions can tangibly be seen. It comes to light when you believe and hope so firmly that you are ready to demolish roofs and ignore angry comments and glances from others. It's when you get up and do everything you can.

For whom or what should you have faith? What roof do you need to demolish? And who could help you do it?

So, instead of just gazing longingly into New Land, grab a couple of your friends and get to work on that roof.

MAKE YOUR OWN BED

The American entrepreneur Gary Hamel said, "You can't use an old map to see a new land." Sometimes New Land will mean a decisive change of course in our lives. You have to leave the old behind and consciously close doors behind you.

Some of the disciples had been fishermen before their time with Jesus. When he was suddenly gone, it left a vacuum in their lives and they fell back into old habits. "Simon Peter said, 'I'm going fishing!' The others said, 'We will go with you'" (John 21:3, CEV). They seem to have kept their fishing kits. Things were different with Elisha; when he was called to be a prophet, he was completely occupied with his old life, ploughing his field with a couple of yokes of oxen. When he entered New Land, he started a fire with the wooden yokes and grilled the oxen on it. Maybe that seems a little extreme to you, while someone else would think it's helpful – it all depends on your personality and life circumstances. Socrates said, "The secret of change is to focus all your energy not on fighting the old, but on building the new." This practical tip can help us to discover the secret of a successful search for New Land. It looks forward in hope instead of getting stuck looking backward.

Before we set off for New Land, we first need to consciously let go of the Old Land that holds us back. It could be dreams and wishes that God did not intend for us, an incorrect self-image, or even prayers that we have already decided how God should answer. Sometimes it is a past we cannot get away from that has come to define our present.

One of my students always used to become completely paralysed whenever I gave him instructions. When I asked him about it, he told me that a teacher had once told him that he was stupid and would never amount to anything. Those words had burned their way into his heart, and he started to believe them deep down. He couldn't get out of that Old Land until he understood the source of his paralysis and the fact that the teacher had been completely wrong about him. Unfortunately, I meet so many people who are hanging on to paralysing Old Land like it was a lifebuoy. We are all pros when it comes to clinging to the familiar, even if it isn't helpful.

On one of his missionary journeys, Peter arrived in Lydda one day, where he met Aeneas, who had been bedridden for eight years. After my back operation last summer, I spent a couple of days in bed in the hospital. That sterile hospital smell and the food that all tasted the same had me in a bit of a huff in no time. "Peter said to Aeneas, 'Jesus Christ has healed you! Get up and make up your bed.' Right away he stood up" (Acts 9:34, CEV).

It sounds to me like that man had a pretty good thing going and had got used to it; maybe he had resigned himself to his situation. It may even have been easy for him to have others "make the bed" for him. And then he gets healed, but that's not all – he's supposed to make his own bed too! What an important message that we need to hear, too. Wherever we have resigned ourselves to our limitations, where those boundaries have become comfortable, that is where Jesus comes in and says, "Get up and make up your bed." He requires us to stop feeling sorry for ourselves and to stop giving excuses why we are not able to follow him.

Our hands and arms are only free to embrace the new when we have let go of the old. Hands that are already full and holding on tightly are unable to receive the new things God wants to give. We cling to things that we love and want more than anything to hang on to. It may be an unhealthy relationship, possessions, a particular lifestyle, or specific ideas about faith. In the end, we are just holding on to Old Land like Aeneas and his mat, and we don't even realize that we are stuck.

I was in a band with some friends when I was younger and, being Swiss, we always dreamed of hitting it big and performing abroad. Just when we got our first invitation to perform at a festival in Germany, the other band members felt it was time to quit. I could not understand them at all because the band was part of my dream. In the end, I had to let it go. I went to the festival anyway, and I was asked to preach. That was the unexpected start of my international preaching ministry. I had to sacrifice the good in order to receive the best, but I would not have been willing to do that because I was clinging to my beloved Old Land.

We need to relax our hands and let go. Our inability to do so is often because we are unable to imagine that God knows us better than we know ourselves and that he really wants the best for us. We don't trust that he has really prepared "good works" for us and placed them along our path.

I learned an important lesson about letting go the hard way. We were with a wild group of hobby athletes in Ticino in the sunny south of Switzerland, looking for any available adrenaline kick. One day was dedicated to water sports, and we went tubing behind a speedy motorboat. At some point my competitive self took over, and I vowed to win the tube rodeo by staying on the longest. I held onto that tube for dear life.

The first couple of minutes were no problem, but when the motorboat took a curve, things got a bit hairy. My tube crossed the wake of the boat and I bounced into the air a few times. At one point, the tube flipped over, and I was hanging on from below. But not for long. The force of the water was a total surprise. My wide-open mouth was flooded, my head was jerked back, and my arms stretched out like on a medieval torture rack. When I finally came up, now quite a distance from my tube, I was sure I would need to spend the rest of the day with a snorkel looking for my fingers and my bottom jaw. Now I know: sometimes it's not worth hanging on like an idiot.

**Are you prepared to let go of your entrenched ideas?
Or will you choose to do it the hard way?**

Letting go of Old Land also involves doing away with aspects of your faith that are no longer alive. I meet lots of people who have been walking with Christ for years, and when they arrive in midlife their faith suddenly crumbles before their eyes. Sometimes it is caused by a marital crisis or problems in the family. They end up wondering whether God ever saw them, who he really is, what, if anything, of their image of God is true, whether he really exists, and what all the religious stuff that they wanted to emulate for so long is supposed to be about anyway. The problem is that they have clung to things that were no longer alive. It's like building a Lego house. Lots of people pitch in to build your house, often spicing things up with special pieces, things that you've never really thought through: "God is love", "Heaven is wonderful", "A Christian is nice", or "You're not allowed to have problems in your marriage". The result is that the foundation is sparse and the upper layers have a lot of add-ins that you have never firmed up for yourself; it's all quite wonky. I suggest that you identify these wonky bits and have the courage to take them out completely. What is up there on that tower that you haven't really ever said yes to completely? It's not wrong to ask the hard questions about faith; maybe you'll even need to go all the way back to the beginning in some areas. God can take it. Then you can put all the pieces back in place, but only the ones that you truly agree with. This will make your faith authentic and stable. And, in the end, alive.

Where is God calling you to let go of Old Land? For example, things, ideas, expectations, ideals that you have sunk your teeth into? Where have you become too comfortable or fearful to let go? Take a little trip inside yourself and look into the future.

Relax, lean back (or maybe you'd prefer to sit on the edge of a 10-metre-high wall somewhere), and imagine yourself in five or ten years from now. What do you want your life to look like?

What if you could freeze your current life so that everything would be exactly the same in ten years – your job, hobbies, family – except that you would have got older? What things would you want to keep and what would you get rid of?

You will only have the chance to discover the New Land that awaits you when you are ready to break away from the coast where you are sitting and feeling bored.

COME OUT

Discovering New Land often has to do with the rediscovery of Old Land. This might sound totally contradictory since you may have just had a breakthrough and decided to let go of the Old Land that disrupts and slows you down. But in the Bible, it is not a question of either/or, but of as well as. So, in this area, there is not only one direction in which we can move. We are called to discover both New Land as well as Old Land.

But not all Old Land is worth rediscovering. As I just wrote, there are some places that I need to decide to leave because that ground is no longer appropriate for the next phase of my life or because it's simply not what God intends for me. At the same time, there is also Old Land that God does intend for me, but, for whatever reason, I gave it up, left, and lost sight of it.

One of my favourite Bible stories is when Jesus spectacularly raises his friend Lazarus from the dead (John 11). This story is the source of the term Lazarus Effect (also known as Lazarus taxon) and refers to the re-emergence of animals that were determined to be extinct. There are many seal species that had been considered extinct since the nineteenth century and were then rediscovered more than a hundred years later. The Laotian rock rat was only known from fossils until a few years ago in Khammouan, Laos, when a scientist stumbled across a couple of grilled ones at a market.[28] The Utila iguana was rediscovered at the end of the twentieth century after scientists had searched for it for about one hundred years. I am fascinated by the numerous species of birds, fish, insects, and amphibians that were thought to be extinct, until they suddenly reappeared. Sometimes we also rediscover things which we had assumed were long dead. It is important to keep these things alive and not to make the same mistake as David Lyall, a lighthouse keeper from New Zealand, and his cat Tibbles. Tibbles was the one who discovered a new species of bird in 1894, the Lyall's wren. Unfortunately, that local species could not fly, so Tibbles went down in history for two spectacular achievements simultaneously. He not only discovered the wren, but according to the story, he wiped out the species, too. In Tibbles' defence, one should also mention that there were a lot of other stray cats on that island. At least you can see fifteen preserved examples of Lyall's wren – a bit tattered and dishevelled thanks to Tibbles – in various museums today.[29]

Sometimes we rediscover things that we lost along the way through life: dreams, abilities, light-heartedness, a certain way of believing things. If you open yourself to discovering New Land, you will inevitably also learn to see Old Land through new eyes.

In a certain phase of my life, I lost my passion for God's Word. I had started reading things out of habit, then out of duty, and then not at all, until I rediscovered the joy of reading the Bible by studying it with friends. Together, we saw the power of the Bible and how much of it is applicable to our daily lives.

Each and every evening we spent together was an inspiration and an encouragement that motivated me to retake that Old Land for myself.

Maybe you have experienced highs and lows in your prayer life – you only pray because you want something from God. And then you stop praying altogether for a while, because you feel like your prayers don't do anything anyway. Prayer became alive for me, just like Lazarus coming out of the tomb, when I realized that it is a foundational component of the relationship between me and God. It's not about achieving a specific purpose, but it's primarily about the relationship.

Sometimes we just let things go in life and lose ground in the process – just like the church at Ephesus. In Revelation 2, God praises them as a great congregation that is involved and has done a lot of good. But then we read this stinging statement: "But I have this against you: you have abandoned the passionate love you had for me at the beginning" (Revelation 2:4, TPT). Here, in our relationship with God, in the special intimacy he intends for us to have with him, it is easy for us to lose ground. That's generally true of all relationships. During the early stages of my relationship with Tamara, I could hardly wait to receive her promised email in my inbox. Those farewells on the train platform after a weekend together were so hard. I had to travel seven hours by train to sit with her in a café for an hour – and she had to skip school to do that. When I was at university, I worked in her parents' vineyard for two weeks and asked them to pay my wages into her account so that she could buy herself a few nice but unnecessary things. That first love was palpable. Now, when Tamara asks me to bring her something sweet from the kitchen, the answer is usually something like, "Oh, I'm so comfortable here. But if you're going, then bring me something, too!"

When you get too comfortable, that blazing fire starts to go out and at some point you are left with faintly glimmering coals. Or maybe the fire dies completely. That's why God tells us to "repent and do the works of love [we] did at first" in Revelation 2:5 (TPT). If you want to have an intimate, heartfelt relationship with God, then you don't need to wait until he comes down to meet you or until emotions fall down from heaven right into your lap. You can get things started by actively opening up and doing works of love. Don't finish praying when you have asked for everything you want and need, but keep going. Don't just invest your designated hours, but spend some more time with God. It works the same in relationships, even in a marriage. Your heart and your emotions follow your works of love.

Where have you already lost Old Land in your life that you were not supposed to give up? Where would you like to regain territory?

Maybe it's time to turn around, to admit where you messed up, and to repent for things you did or did not do. Repentance is about recognizing and then confessing things that were wrong or not good and then turning away from them.

What is keeping you from starting anew today?

Jesus stands before the dead areas of your life, in front of lost Old Land, and calls out in a loud voice: "Lazarus, come out!" Dare to step into New Land.

12

COSMIC

Living in New Land

Regardless of the time of year, the Christmas story always has something to tell us. We see the Wise Men set off on a journey based on their trust in a couple of astrological signs. Without really believing in God, they have confidence in the heavenly signals. After a long journey, they arrive in the place they have been heading to – and hoping for – for so long, and they sense that the tiny person lying in a manger at their feet must be the sought-after king. Not particularly irritated by the unroyal decor of the stable, they give Jesus the treasures brought from afar. They have discovered their New Land. Instead of returning to King Herod to give their report as he commanded, they trust a message in a dream and take the scenic route home. I'm impressed to see how these men, even in their moment of greatest success and after an unbelievably long journey to get there in the first place, do not become careless, but continue to trust in heavenly leading.

It is especially important in times of success not to live off the success itself, but to continue to trust in God. If the Wise Men had acted differently – perhaps thoughtlessly or with a bit less presence of mind – then the entire Christmas story would have ended badly. If they had returned to Herod and drawn him a map with the location of the stable, the evangelists wouldn't have had much to write about. That would have brought an abrupt end to one of the most amazing stories of all time – about a God who becomes a human being. The three Wise Men would have become the Three Stooges in world history who, by their stupidity, successfully managed to sabotage God's unique liberation plan.

The Newlandic lifestyle means staying in touch with God and focusing on him – through both successes and failures.

KEEP GOING TO NEW LAND

One of the biggest hindrances to success in life is giving up too soon. When God has put something in your future, he will also make sure that you are able to reach it. And you shouldn't quit striving for it, regardless of the setbacks you experience.

Thomas Edison is an unbelievable inspiration to me in this respect. He was born in a small town in northern Ohio on 11 February 1847. Even in his early years he battled a hearing impairment. But because he pursued his goal relentlessly and undeterred, he shaped history like few others, with some 1,100 US patents. In 1882 alone, he submitted 114 applications for new inventions. Many were historic milestones, while others, like a piano or furniture made of cement, didn't really take off with consumers.

The best part of Edison's story to me is the way he approached the problem of the electric lightbulb. Lots of inventors before him had failed to develop a product that could outperform the gas lamp. The lightbulb had to be durable, odourless, and flicker-free, emit little heat, be able to be switched on and off, and be operated by one power source. Some physicists considered the problem unsolvable – but not Edison.

However, the path to successfully inventing the lightbulb was paved with setbacks. The entire development process is said to have filled 40,000 pages of notes. He tested different materials to find the perfect filament. No one knows for certain how many attempts it took, but if we suppose that he succeeded on the 10,000th try, that means there were 9,999 more or less unsuccessful tries preceding it. It would have been a shame had he given up at attempt 7,438 – or even worse at 9,999! In any case, he is said to have remarked after thousands of unsuccessful attempts, "I have not failed. I've just found 10,000 ways that won't work."

Other quotes from Edison are completely applicable to our situation today; for example: "Our greatest weakness lies in giving up. The most certain way to succeed is always to try just one more time."

Keeping going is one of the prerequisites for Edison's success. Don't be discouraged by setbacks if you feel you are on the right track. You can't learn to ice skate without falling down. Many of the truly significant successes in your life will only be visible in the long run. For example, I can't raise my children in just one week – it's about keeping at it over many years. A friendship or a marriage is not established with one kiss; rather, it takes a life-long process of walking together day by day. That is exactly why we shouldn't give up and bury our dreams halfway down the path.

For me, Caleb is the Thomas Edison of the Bible, not because he was such a great inventor, but because he kept going and didn't give up. Some forty-five years after receiving the promise of a specific piece of land, he showed up to claim it from God.

So I'm asking you for the hill country that the Lord promised me that day. You were there. You heard the other spies talk about that part of the hill country and the large, walled towns where the Anakim live. But maybe the Lord will help me take their land, just as he promised.
(Joshua 14:12, CEV)

If Caleb had focused on his circumstances, at some point in all those years he would certainly have given up and buried the dream of having his own land. There were many battles to fight and sometimes it seemed endless. But Caleb held on to the promise and became the first of the tribes to receive land. At that time, he was eighty-five years old and could easily have asked for a cosy little piece of land with a jacuzzi and a fridge with an integrated ice dispenser after all those battles. Instead, the land he chose was anything but cosy and not at all easy to possess: it was up in the mountains where the Anakim "giants" lived and the cities were more like fortresses. Everyone within hearing distance probably winced when they heard where Caleb wanted to go. And they probably let out a collective sigh of relief knowing that he would get that inhospitable plot and not them.

At Christmas one year we played a familiar gift game with our relatives. Everyone wrapped up something they wanted to get rid of and brought it along. Then we started rolling the dice to see who got to choose first. Each person could choose from the unopened parcels or steal something that someone else had already opened. A couple of gifts were quickly identified as very popular and hotly contested, while others were labelled by the group as the booby prize and avoided at all costs. Everyone was glad not to get that one. That is what it must have felt like back then: "Thank God, Caleb got that desolate piece of New Land." Still, everyone probably respected him greatly for having the courage to take that piece of land.

Caleb held on so firmly to the original promise that even a "maybe" was enough: "But maybe the Lord will help me take their land" (Joshua 14:12, CEV). I don't always know where God is taking me; I may have an inkling, but he doesn't always speak in unmistakably clear tones. I have seldom woken up in the morning to see the answer to my prayer written on the wall in chocolate-milk ink. But something I do try to do is follow a promise or that sense of inner peace like Caleb did. "Maybe God has prepared this for me," and then I test that "maybe". I have also learned that it is often enough that "maybe" God is with me. If I don't find him for certain in the "maybe", then I just make a course correction and continue on. Naturally, God won't ever just withdraw from us and leave us standing alone. In Isaiah 46:4, he says, "I will still be the same when you are old and grey, and I will take care of you. I created you. I will carry you and always keep you safe" (CEV).

God keeps working on you for a lifetime, and you should hang on to him and his dreams for you. Be like Thomas Edison, who wasn't deterred by setbacks, and have the courage of Caleb to ask God for specific things and to keep going, even if you can only say that "maybe" he is with you. God's blessing could be waiting for you behind every "maybe".

Or maybe it is time for you to restart something you stopped doing a long time ago. Twenty-year-old Shizo Kanakuri stood at the starting line for the Olympic marathon in 1912 in Stockholm.[30] For him, you could say it was one marathon after another, because he already had an eighteen-day journey fraught with difficulties behind him. He had taken a ship from Tokyo to Vladivostok, then transferred to the Trans-Siberian railroad to travel through Russia and Finland to his final destination in Stockholm. Afterwards, he needed five days to recover.

For track and field fans in Sweden, the Olympics were the biggest event they had ever seen; some 20,000 people filled the stadium and thousands lined the route to watch the marathon. However, the unusually high temperature of 25°C caused problems for the organizers as well as the athletes. Of the ninety-eight registered runners, only sixty-nine actually started the race, and only thirty-five finished. The Portuguese athlete Francisco Lázaro even died trying. A couple of days later, Shizo Kanakuri was also declared dead by authorities when he disappeared and could not be found anywhere. The first Japanese athlete who started the marathon had simply got lost. Everyone assumed he was just another marathon victim.

In reality, at kilometre 30, Kanakuri had been invited into a local spectator's garden for something to drink. As he was ready to keel over, he accepted the invitation, had something to drink, and promptly fell asleep due to extreme exhaustion. He didn't wake up until the next day. The Olympic Games had already finished, and because he was so embarrassed by what had happened, he returned to Japan alone without notifying anyone of his departure. Fifty-five years later, at the age of seventy-five, the now retired university professor Kanakuri returned to finish the marathon from the place he had stopped back in 1912, thus completing the longest marathon ever with a time of 54 years, 8 months, 6 days, 8 hours, 32 minutes and 20.3 seconds. That's a speed of 8.4 centimetres per hour; it's tempting to say "at a snail's pace", but the snails in my garden can move up to 3 metres in an hour, so that would have left Kanakuri in the dust.

As he said himself, it was a long trip. During his personal race, he had got married and had six children and ten grandchildren. That's quite an accomplishment.

Is there anything you gave up a long time ago – either willingly or unwillingly? With a lot of things, it's never too late and you're never too old to finish what you started. If it really is New Land that God has prepared for you, then you can restart your race at the point where you stopped. Keep going!

DEDICATE YOURSELF TO TRUTH

One challenge as we try to keep going is that we don't long for truth as much as we'd like to think. Sometimes our longing for comfort wins. We even accept that we could be fooling ourselves about a particular situation or people, just because it's more convenient to do so. However, truth is a fundamental characteristic of Newlandic culture. If we are not truthful with ourselves, other people, or even God, then we are an obstacle on the path to New Land.

We see these two opposing sides in Jehoshaphat, king of Judah and Ahab, king of Israel (2 Chronicles 18 and 1 Kings 22). The two were related by marriage, and one day, Ahab wanted to convince Jehoshaphat to join him in attacking Ramoth in Gilead. Somehow he thought that going to war together would deepen their fledgling bromance. Jehoshaphat jumped on the bandwagon immediately, but he wanted to know what God thought about their plan. That is never a bad idea when you are facing an important decision. So Ahab called 400 prophets together and they confirmed the plan unanimously: "Yes! God will help you capture the city" (2 Chronicles 18:5, CEV).

That would have been enough for most people; but Jehoshaphat wasn't impressed by numbers. He wondered, instead, whether there was a "real prophet" available, a prophet of the Lord.

"'We could ask Micaiah son of Imlah,' Ahab said. 'But I hate Micaiah. He always has bad news for me'" (2 Chronicles 18:7, CEV). I just love his statement – it's dripping with truth about how people really think. Ahab didn't want to hear from Micaiah because he told the king unpleasant things. So, instead, he had his 400-man chorus come out to sing him a nice song of lies. He preferred to hear pleasant lies instead of uncomfortable truths.

While Micaiah was being brought before Jehoshaphat and Ahab, the choir cranked up the volume a bit more and continued predicting a great victory. The messenger who was sent to get Micaiah didn't want to ruin the mood, and he tried to instruct Micaiah about what to say: "Micaiah, all the prophets have good news for Ahab. Now go and say the same thing" (2 Chronicles 18:12, CEV). But Micaiah, who was deaf in one ear, simply replied, "I'll say whatever the living Lord my God tells me to say" (2 Chronicles 18:13, CEV).

It was clear for Micaiah that he would not water down or alter the truth. Funnily enough, though, his answer was actually what the king wanted to hear: "Yes! The Lord will help you capture the city" (2 Chronicles 18:14, CEV). He didn't make his statement out of fear; he had already made it clear to the messenger that he wouldn't just tell the king what he wanted to hear. I suppose, though, that the smug grin on Micaiah's lips was enough to tip the king off to the ruse. "Ahab shouted, 'Micaiah, I've told you over and over to tell me the truth! What does the Lord really say?'" (2 Chronicles 18:15, CEV).

So Micaiah began speaking the whole relentless truth: namely, that God did not want them to fight. All Ahab could do was snarl back at Jehoshaphat, "I told you he would bring me bad news!" (2 Chronicles 18:17, CEV).

Micaiah accused the other prophets of lying, which made the prophet Zedekiah quite angry since he had just given everything to convince the king. He even slapped Micaiah in the face, but this didn't deter Micaiah from insisting that he would be proven right by the outcome of the battle.

In the end, Ahab listened to his 400 choir boys, and it ended up being the last time he would need advice from anyone at all. He died in that disastrous battle, which he had talked himself into thinking was God's plan for him. Evidently, it was not.

Perhaps you are sniggering at Zedekiah and his 399 embarrassed colleagues because Micaiah uncovered their pathetic plan to make Ahab happy, to say what he wanted to hear. But we all have similar Zedekiah moments. Once I nodded in approval when someone I really admired started passionately sharing his ideas about the combination of religion and transcendental journeys. I was already in mid-nod when I realized how strange it all was. But because I didn't want to get wrapped up in a long discussion right then, and because I wanted the other person to like me, I just sat there and kept nodding. I had fallen prey to the Zedekiah temptation – saying what someone else wanted to hear.

"You, my people, have sinned in two ways – you have rejected me, the source of life-giving water, and you've tried to collect water in cracked and leaking pits dug in the ground" (Jeremiah 2:13, CEV). Most people have already dug their own substitute water sources that they hope to get a little life out of – to satisfy their thirst just a bit.

What people have become your source? I don't mean a source of inspiration, but one of those substitute sources. Have you fallen into an unhealthy dependency on water from any cracked and leaking pits? Have you left the source altogether in any areas of your life?

If you are trying to be like Zedekiah and make everyone happy all the time so they will like you, you will soon become someone you no longer recognize: a person you probably don't want to be.

And sometimes we are like King Ahab; we really do want to know where God wants us to go in life, but we try to dictate to him how he should answer. We don't want to hear the truth, but the answer that will please us. I call this the Micaiah Complex. It always happens when we reject God's answer and put our own opinion above his. We often prefer to live with a lie rather than deal with the truth honestly. Or, as Ahab would have put it, "I'd rather die than face God's truth." And that's exactly what he did. In his case, the truth really did have a face – namely, Micaiah's.

In what areas of your life are you in danger of telling God how he should answer you? Where have you failed to even bring in a "Micaiah" in the sense that you don't even ask God what he thinks because you are afraid he will tell you something unpleasant?

This is not a plea for you to leave your brains at the door; rather, it is a call not to limit God's access to certain areas of your life because it seems more convenient.

It is so important that we do not allow ourselves to be driven by fear or false motives, but that we strive to find and follow the truth above all. We will always win in the end when we reach out for truth. "Truth is your friend," says Uli Eggers. This releases a lot of life energy, even if it is not always the most comfortable or convenient path.

The four characters in this story represent four different positions that we all tend to move between. I have discovered tendencies of all four in myself. Sometimes I'm an Ahab and I don't want to hear what God has to say. In the past, I've even caught myself acting like Zedekiah, poised to do or say things to please people. The more I listen like Jehoshaphat and speak

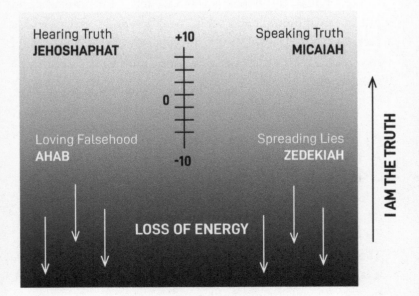

like Micaiah, the more powerful my life becomes. On the Ahab–Zedekiah level you lose so much energy trying to make sure your house of lies doesn't fall in on itself. If you find yourself in a similar situation, then know that the path that leads to growth in Christ, who is himself the truth (John 14:6), is the most liberating.

Where do you see evidence of an Ahab or Zedekiah dynamic in your life? What concrete steps can you take in the next few days to become more like Jehoshaphat and Micaiah?

Incorporating and cultivating the truth in your Newlandic lifestyle will automatically lead you to New Land again and again.

KEEP YOUR EYES ON THE HORIZON

An important component of a Newlandic spirit is keeping your eyes on the horizon. After spending a few weeks on a mission project in Uganda, I had a short break with Tamara on the picturesque island of Zanzibar. We went out to a reef near the beach in a small boat, planning to enjoy snorkelling in an underwater world filled with brilliant colours. As the boat rocked back and forth on the waves, I realized that my body couldn't take it anymore and was unable to compensate for the constant movement. After about half an hour, my face was competing with the coral reef below to see which one had the best shade of green. I tried to save myself by getting into the water, but that really didn't help. My head was floating on the surface, but down below, everything kept moving.

At some point I gave up – just before my snorkel filled up with something other than air.

When I got back into the boat, I wanted to eat something, hoping to settle my stomach, but the only things I found on board were watermelon and bananas. Since beggars can't be choosers, I stuffed half a watermelon and two bananas into my mouth as I tried to stay focused on the horizon. A bit groggy, I heard everyone cry out with joy as a pod of dolphins came up around our little boat. My fellow snorkellers all jumped into the water to swim with the dolphins, certainly an amazing experience. But I just had to stay in the rocking boat, holding on to my seat, trying to keep the banana–watermelon cocktail down. No one had said anything about feeding dolphins when I booked the snorkelling excursion. Normally I would have been excited to see those creatures, but in that moment they only annoyed me because it was all I could do to keep myself focused on the horizon. There was one hyperactive dolphin that kept jumping up into my line of sight. In the end, however, focusing on the horizon saved me from worse trouble.

When things get stormy in life and everything starts to rock back and forth, there is only one thing that helps: the Horizon Perspective. Many things in life are only made bearable by keeping our eyes on the horizon – just like seasickness in a boat. When loved ones die and we have to let them go, it would be inconsolable to think that there was nothing else afterwards. For people who know Christ, death is like a colon, a punctuation mark that is always followed by something more. Our lives together will resume when we meet again beyond the horizon. Even when you find yourself in a phase of life that forces you to admit that there are things you will never experience or achieve, the Horizon Perspective will help. When I realize that I have got too old to do a triple flip on the trampoline, when I wish I could have spent more time with a loved one who passed away, when I am forced to live with illness or other limitations… without the Horizon Perspective and without looking forward to what comes after, everything would be unbearably hopeless.

When I was a child, I always heard the phrases, "If we're still alive, God willing," and "As long as Jesus doesn't come back first." Somehow I miss that way of thinking today. We shouldn't give up on life and just sit around waiting for Jesus and heaven to appear. But it is still good not to lose that Horizon Perspective, because it gives our lives the right outlook, allowing the sound of hope to echo through even the roughest storms of life.

I have also experienced a kind of spiritual seasickness of the soul. The feeling of nausea at sea comes from our brain trying, and failing, to balance everything out. The brain gets overloaded with different, contrary sensory messages coming in simultaneously. The same thing happens in life. There is an everyday reality that we consider to be the maximum reality, and then comes eternity, which we can't quite pin down. If we do not keep our eyes fixed on a stable horizon, the brain gets confused, producing the feeling of nausea.

When we think of New Land, we need to move the hope that we have as Christians back into the centre again. In our twenty-first century European culture and lifestyle with all its amenities, our faith is extremely focused on the here and now. We have almost completely lost sight of something that Jesus spoke about frequently: the coming kingdom. In all our faith efforts and everyday adventures, we sometimes forget that we are only passing through as strangers (Psalm 119:19, CEV) and our lives are moving toward something that is far greater than anything we can imagine – something that we, as foreigners here, should be on the lookout for (Hebrews 11:13, CEV).

It is an exhilarating thought to know that this life continues seamlessly into the next; to know that I am not missing out on anything in this life that I won't have more than enough time for in the next. I will be able to try out or continue all the things I can't do in this limited world at some point in the future. In Hebrews 13:14, we read, "For we have no city here on earth to be our permanent home, but we seek the city that is destined to come" (TPT). I like this verse, but even for people who are familiar with Newlandic culture, it often seems a bit over the top. Many people don't really long for heaven. We want to live to a ripe old age, we cling to the here and now, and we only long for what we can experience here. I don't usually wake up in the morning with an overpowering sense of longing for "the city that is destined to come". I have set up my life quite nicely here, and I would probably be more disappointed than pleased if I received my notification of immediate departure this evening.

This is a first-world problem, because we can afford to live – long and well. On my trips to poorer places around the world, I realized that the hope for a future is much stronger and more evident. And that heavenly perspective brings hope and the joy of anticipation into the now. Some may find it odd, naive, or just ridiculous to focus on eternity; but, actually, it's even more naive and ridiculous not to. The relationship between life and eternity speaks clearly. If this book represented eternity, then your life now would only have got as far as the first letter on the first page. But we don't need to develop a death wish or walk through life with a ridiculously naive perspective. Still, it is good for us not to lose sight of the big picture. Only the integration of our future brings the right dynamic into the present and fills it with an undertone of joy that should be noticeable among our ranks.

At a recent conference, a journalist asked me question after question. When I tried to gently hint that I needed to be going, she put down her pen with a look of mild desperation and said, "I'm not asking for the newspaper anymore. I have more questions of my own. Why is everybody here so happy? Does everybody have to be happy here?" She had picked up on what lives in us despite our circumstances through the Horizon Perspective: the undertone of joy and hope in life. Sometimes I feel like we have been placed at the entrance to the world's greatest amusement park with breathtaking rollercoasters, beautiful gardens, restaurants that would make your mouth water… and we drop off all our energy, joy, frustration, and every question at the turnstile by the entrance. We try to pass through with as little resistance as possible, bargaining over the ticket price and getting upset with everyone who tries to jump the queue. While we are waiting, we get an ice cream in an attempt to distract ourselves from our own impatience, we try to peek over the fence at the natural beauty inside, and we try spinning around a bit to give ourselves that carousel feeling. But, in reality, we have lost our perspective completely. We will only have to wait an instant at the turnstile – five minutes at the most. And our ticket for the park has no time limit at all. So stop focusing on the turnstile! Even if it doesn't feel like it to you, eternal life is a reality, just like your life here and now.

It helps me to live with a Newlandic spirit that looks at things from the heavenly perspective. When I get upset about something in my daily life, looking toward heaven actually helps me put things back into the right perspective quite often. The things to come help me relax my expectations of life. Because I know that things will not simply stop one day, but will, instead, finally get started in earnest, I don't live with the constant need to get as much as possible out of every moment of my life. That's so exhausting! It reminds me of trying to suck the very last drop out of a carton of juice with my straw – and the horrible noise it makes. Not to mention how annoying it is for everyone around you who has to listen to it.

The Newlandic Horizon Perspective helps you to live a pleasant and calm life, far from the urge to experience everything and to have everything perfect.

FOLLOW THE WATER

The Ténéré desert is not the first place that comes to mind when you think of flashy pool parties, where people relax with ice-cold drinks and enjoy the sun. Instead, it is a glowing oven where temperatures often reach above 50°C during the day and fall below zero at night. If it rotated slowly, you would almost think you had ended up in some kind of gigantic microwave. This part of the southern Sahara is called the "Desert of all Deserts", and the sun-bleached camel humps testify to the fact that few things survive here. That's what made one acacia tree so unique.

It stood alone in the middle of the Ténéré desert, which spans over 400,000 km². Locals had known about the tree for decades. It was equally worshipped and feared because its mere existence in the middle of this hellish fiery furnace seemed other-worldly in the least. "You must see the tree to believe its existence," noted Michel Lesourd, Commander of the Allied Military Mission stationed in French West Africa on 21 May 1939.[31] How had the loneliest tree in the world survived there for so many years?

In 1973, drivers in the Citroën Desert Rally found the tree had died. Its demise is shrouded in mystery. It is certainly possible that a violent desert storm snapped its trunk. Locals tell the tale of a drunken driver ploughing into the tree with his lorry. Another version goes back much further. In 1939, the French army wanted to solve the mystery of how the tree could survive such harsh conditions in the desert, so they began digging a well right next to the tree. They shovelled for months without success – the only redeeming moment was when they were able to grill an unfortunate bird that had died of heat exhaustion and landed next to the tree. After nine months and a legendary depth of 35 metres they finally hit groundwater – and the roots of the tree. Roots as tall as the Christ the Redeemer statue in Rio de Janeiro. And more than eleven times deeper than the height of the tree itself. The 3-metre-high tree was probably the last remnant of an earlier oasis that was swallowed up by the desert, but that tree's roots followed the water as it passed through the ground to the water source.

And the stupidest part: when the well was being dug, some of the roots were cut off. This, they supposed, was the reason the tree died many years later.

There are also times in New Land when you find yourself in completely foreign and inhospitable terrain. You have been given a task for which you seem to lack all the necessary skills, or you are faced with a life situation that you have no experience to master – a diagnosis of infertility, the departure of important people in your company, a teenage daughter with an eating disorder, or perhaps an exciting new opportunity that you'd like to try but have simply never done before. You may also find yourself in a stage of life where you are quite lonely and there is no one in sight who can help you. Just like that acacia tree, you are living in the middle of a life-threatening desert. Your survival depends on whether you have managed to follow the water faithfully. Since it sinks down even further underground during difficult times, it allows you to grow your roots even deeper so that you can withstand the storms that come without being damaged. You have a firm footing.

Following this simple spiritual principle makes you like the tree from Psalm 1 that is planted next to a stream, bears fruit, and always has leaves. "Those people succeed in everything they do" (Psalm 1:3, CEV). The text says that a deep longing for God's Word is the requirement for such a tree and that we think about it "day and night". That means your faith roots have to grow deeper. This image is all about your relationship with God so that you spend time with him and continually follow his truths. It's like in a marriage: you don't only do nice things, little acts of love, because you long to be with the other person. You know that doing nice things and acts of love helps feelings of longing for the other person to grow. That is how love is renewed.

Of course, you may also sleep at night; you don't have to meditate on God's Word 24/7. Ultimately, the idea is that everything in our lives is filled with divine truth and our relationship to God. God and his Word should not simply be a note in the margin of your life, or like footnotes in a book. A healthy spiritual life is evident to those around you. There is a difference between the worship leader talking every Sunday morning about how he marvels at nature (something he is certainly allowed to do) and sharing biblical truth from a powerful, dynamic spiritual life that fills his worship.

We have to realize that we are swimming against the tide of today's zeitgeist and fast-food culture. We have got used to not digging deep in so many areas of our lives; instead, we are satisfied with roots that stay close to the surface. This also applies to our spiritual lives. Whether locally or online, today everyone has access to church services with messages from the world's best speakers. We sit like squirrels on a pile of nuts, with more food than we could ever possibly digest. So we end up swallowing a lot of it undigested, which can lead to spiritual bloating. We read the Bible in high-speed mode, a few seconds for a verse or two on the smartphone. Spending thirty minutes with a particular word or a longer passage once in a while to see what God wants to show us is already foreign to us. But these would often be the moments when we could reach out to God and drive our roots deeper.

What about planning a specific time to meditate this week? Choose a place where nothing and no one will interrupt you, put your phone in flight mode, and then take time to have fellowship with God and to consider a specific Bible verse or passage. Psalm 1 would certainly be a good place to start.

Drive your roots deeper. If there were a list of spiritual tips, then this one would be in the Top Five without a doubt: follow the water. Let the roots of your heart grow deeper and deeper, following the living water wherever it flows.

FUTU RIST IC

The Epilogue

We live in a complicated world that is constantly becoming even more complex. This development can already be seen in the Bible. All of world history begins in a garden and will end in a golden city. Life is evolving more and more from simplicity into unbelievable intricacy. As Christians, we need to continue developing as well. It is definitely correct and important to live with an awareness of history. But sometimes we make wrong decisions about which things should be preserved and when the time for New Land has come.

A second point is even more devastating: we have ceased to believe that the simplicity of Jesus is the answer to the complex challenges of our society. Many Christians have lost their confidence in the gospel, without even noticing. This is the gospel that Paul explains by saying, "The message about the cross doesn't make any sense to lost people. But for those of us who are being saved, it is God's power at work" (1 Corinthians 1:18, CEV).

Jesus said that he is the "light of the world" (John 8:12, NIV) – he is the light not just of a couple of religious people, naive simpletons, a particular religion, a specific geographic region, a few nostalgic Westerners... He is the light of the world. Then he went a step further and chose us as his representatives to shine that light into our world: "You are the light of the world" (Matthew 5:14, NIV). We have been given the task of carrying hope into society – or at least into our own little worlds. We should not underestimate the importance of this task. Whenever a society, an organization, or a group faces a particular challenge, it automatically becomes true that whoever spreads hope leads. Especially in times of change, such as those we are facing to an unprecedented extent today, it is essential that the church raise her voice of hope above the fray. And I do not mean hope in the sense of "I hope the weather will be better tomorrow than it was today". Hebrews 6:19 speaks of hope as a strong and secure anchor. Hope is not a desperate last resort, but a deep conviction of the reality of that which is not yet visible; it is a direct fruit of faith.

Hope is the driving force of life. My children do not yet know hopelessness – Papa can still fix everything. If a toy gets broken, bring it to Papa, and he can glue it back together. If a little sister gets hurt, Papa can put her back together, too. Papa can do anything! The same kind of attitude toward our heavenly Father would do us a lot of good, too. The only thing that can keep us going long term is hope. If I didn't have the hope that I could do something positive each day, I probably would not even get out of bed in the morning. If I didn't have any hope that my Indian cooking skills could get better, I would have given up after my last pitiful attempt, the result of which was so inedible that we had to bin it. If my girls lost all hope after their first unsuccessful attempts to learn to ride a bicycle, they would never learn to do it. Hope is what keeps us going. And it is worthwhile to cling to it: "So now we must cling tightly to the hope that lives within us, knowing that God always keeps his promises!" (Hebrews 10:23, TPT).

In his 1942 book, *Voodoo Death*, Walter Cannon examines cases of people who died from things that are not even fatal. Some died from snakebites even though the snake was not poisonous, but they had mistakenly believed it was. People died in situations that threw them into a state of absolute hopelessness so that they came to see death as an unavoidable consequence. The psychobiologist Curt P. Richter followed this line of thinking and performed a series of experiments on rats.[32] He placed them in smooth-walled glass containers, which were impossible to climb out of, and filled them with water, forcing them to swim. Many rats drowned within the first fifteen minutes, although they are quite good swimmers. A few rats were removed from the water shortly before drowning. After they had recovered, they were returned to the water. These rats swam for up to eighty hours – 320 times longer. Experiencing that rescue was a real possibility generated so much hope that they were able to hang on for a long time. The others, who assumed that there was no escape from that glass container, gave in to their inevitable fate and drowned. If we lose hope, we will die. And if you have lost hope in a particular area of your life or for a relationship, then it is also doomed to die.

This Resignation Syndrome can be seen everywhere. Since the early 2000s in Sweden, multiple refugee children have fallen into a coma-like state of physical rigidity (called Resignation Syndrome) after their families were denied asylum and faced being forcibly repatriated to their home countries. A society without hope will collapse on itself. A church that can no longer be the voice of hope in the world will choke on its own lack of identity. On the other hand, hope is an unbelievable source of strength that God has also placed in us.

We need hope to live just as we need air to breathe. Especially in deadlocked and hopeless situations, the broad Horizon Perspective we have in and through Christ is a hope that deeply influences and sustains our lives.

In what areas has hopelessness crept into your life? Which of your relationships feels like a glass container filled with water? Where do you need to keep swimming a bit longer? Or would you be able to hold on to the

hand that is waiting to rescue you from that situation? Do you speak hope into your relationships and situations? To whom could you bring hope? In what concrete ways?

Do not give up or stop clinging to hope. Regardless of how small the spark has become, it is still enough to set entire forests on fire. Hope is more contagious than any epidemic. And the hopeful yearning to hear the call "Land ahoy!" is enough to help you survive the wind and rain of the coming storm.

Real hope is something solid and substantial. The hope of eternity is not made up of chubby cherubs resting on bubblegum-pink clouds. It exists because Jesus gave up his life in a cruel and inhumane way for you and me on the cross. Stained by blood and spit, his body covered with open wounds, the image of Jesus' crucifixion challenges us to really think about the price of our salvation. Dark, frustrating, and disturbing – it is far from a feel-good romance. But it was exactly this irrational situation that brought a new dimension of hope into our world that cannot be compared with anything else.

Hopelessness also means a lack of identity that automatically causes a great deal of collateral damage and throws everything in society out of kilter. When hope is absent in Europe, it is not only about the failure of the church as a neutral institution or the state or a particular financial system or a refugee agency that has collapsed. When hope is absent in Europe, then I have failed as a Christian. Me, personally. I have failed to live out my Newlandic identity, which God has given me. The hopelessness of the people around me stems from my own laziness in following Jesus. The lack of hope for each individual around me grows out of my own lack of identity in Christ. Now, this doesn't mean I have to chasten myself with a belt until my back is wounded and bloody; rather, I can simply allow myself to fall into Jesus' arms. Christ in me cannot fail. But I don't always give him enough space, and I fail to live out my identity as someone who brings hope.

As Christians we know the life of our Christ, but we often do not identify with him enough.

I once read that the Baptist theologian Harvey Cox asked the following question during a lecture to an audience of 600 Christian physicians, therapists, and pastors. He was speaking on the story of the woman with the flow of blood, and he asked the audience members to think about which individual character or group in the story they identified with most. I liked the idea, so I tried it with a group in Germany. There were about 3,000 Christians in the audience when we read the same passage in Luke 8:40–56. Afterwards, I asked people to stand according to which person in the story they could identify with most. A few dozen put themselves with the observers or mourners; even more identified with Jairus' daughter. A couple of hundred identified with Jairus and the woman with the flow of blood; but the majority felt closest to the disciples – as I expected. When I asked them at the end who identified with Jesus, a handful of people stood up. That was Cox's experience, too. Only six people chose Jesus, although in that group of physicians and therapists, the topic of healing should have been a top concern.

We often forget that Christlikeness is our life's goal (Romans 8:29) and that hope does not come from somewhere outside ourselves; rather, it already lives and pulses in us.

Romans 15:13 says, "Now may God, the inspiration and fountain of hope, fill you to overflowing with uncontainable joy and perfect peace as you trust in him. And may the power of the Holy Spirit continually surround your life with his super-abundance until you radiate with hope!" (TPT). I love this powerful verse. It seems to me that Paul has crammed in all the big words he can think of, like the fully stocked sweet shop I walk past in Zurich airport that nearly sends me into a sugar coma just from looking inside.

God, hope, overflowing, joy, peace, trust, super-abundance, hope, power, Holy Spirit – all in just one verse. Either that is spiritual gluttony or it is one of those verses we are meant to chew on for a while and savour for a long time. I love the idea of the Holy Spirit "continually surrounding my life with his super-abundance" in hope. That means we are moving forward, continually walking and growing, increasing – just as Paul describes.

We also enter New Land daily in terms of hope. Anyone who stops hoping stops believing. And anyone who stops believing stops living. Your life is designed to continually grow richer in hope. It grows, it increases. Either you will focus on all the unanswered prayers, on all the negative things you have had to face in your life, and allow them to rob you of your hope, or you decide to cling to hope even more than before, as it says in Hebrews 10:23.

I wrote this book at a time when major political upheavals were causing a sensational uproar throughout the world. My Facebook feed was littered with a seemingly endless stream of posts filled with frustration and hopelessness. Lots of things seemed to be falling apart. History (even going all the way back to the Israelites) teaches us that good kings follow bad kings, who are followed by good kings, who are followed by bad kings, and so on. But, at the end of every historical cycle, we are left standing here with our own lives. Everything was not and is not as depressing as it sometimes sounds, because you and I are the result of the times we live in. Even if it sometimes feels like society is only going in a downward spiral, the wheel of time does not have endless spokes.

I am not prepared to give up my hope to wait passively until the nebulous darkness engulfs the last flickering candle. On the contrary; the good thing about darkness is that it makes the light seem even brighter. And that's the wonderful task of those who follow Jesus with Newlandic faith.

You bring hope because you have the God of hope in you. Count on him in your life and in world history. Cling to him, the one who makes all things new. Spread hope by blessing others and encouraging them. Never stop bringing them into contact with the God of hope.

Let us hold fast to the reality of this hope and carry it to people everywhere. God is not finished with Europe, he is not finished with this world, but he is waiting and longing for entire nations to return to him and to discover his heart again. For that to happen, we need people to bring hope. Hold on to hope and carry it with you everywhere you go.

A DECISION FOR NEW LAND

Spreading a Newlandic lifestyle of hope and going through life with a Newlandic spirit requires a paradigm shift. God wants to help us discover how to think, feel, act, hope, speak, pray, love, live, and believe in a Newlandic way. But we have to intentionally choose this new way. Lots of things in our lives are put into motion when we make a conscious and courageous choice in one area. The engineer Stanislav Yevgrafovich Petrov is one good example.[33] He served as a lieutenant colonel for the Soviet Air Defence Forces in a nuclear missile silo in the secret city of Serphkhov–15, some 85 km south of Moscow. This was the location of the control centre for the "Oko" early-warning missile-defence system, controlled by a network of satellites. Petrov had developed the computer control system. Even his family did not know the details of his work, and the city was not visible on any map. On 26 September 1983, at the height of the Cold War with the US, both sides had their fingers permanently on the trigger. Since the mid-1970s, two-thirds of the 400 SS-20 "Saber" missiles had been aimed at western Europe – at cities like London, Paris, and Bonn. A single rocket had an explosive force of up to one megaton. In comparison, the "Fat Man" bomb dropped on Nagasaki, Japan in 1945 was fifty times less powerful. The West was also well-armed, and the situation was tense.

While the Oko early-warning system could not prevent an attack, it would give them enough time to launch a counter-attack according to the saying, "turnabout is fair play". On that fateful September evening, Petrov reported for duty as usual, but it would turn out to be anything but a routine shift. Shortly before midnight, the 30-metre-wide screen lit up with huge red letters: "LAUNCH!" The Kosmos 1382 spy satellite had detected a single launch from a US nuclear missile silo. In twenty-five minutes, it would strike somewhere in the Soviet Union. That was just enough time to start the launch sequence for a counter-attack. There in the control room, all 200 pairs of eyes were on Petrov.

NEWLANDIC

Although the Oko system was thought to be infallible, Petrov had a gut feeling that it was a false alarm. "They wouldn't launch just a single missile," he thought. A nuclear attack by the US on the USSR would have hundreds of missiles coming at once. He couldn't be sure, but he followed his instincts. He instructed his co-workers to sit down and continue working, and he informed their commander by telephone that it was a false alarm. As he hung up, the sirens started howling again. The system had detected more missile launches – two, three, four, and five. According to regulations, Petrov should have immediately initiated the launch sequence for a Russian strike. That would have meant 750 million dead, 340 million casualties, and every major city in western Europe wiped out. Warheads would have rained down on North America, Europe, and Asia; 1,124 cities, practically all cities with a population of more than 100,000, would have been destroyed in an instant. The world was never as close to nuclear annihilation as on that night, according to a US disarmament expert. But Petrov followed his gut and avoided the start of World War III and the worldwide chaos that would follow. As things turned out, the satellite signal had probably reacted to sunbeams reflected by cloud cover, misinterpreting the flashes of light as signs of a missile launch below.

Petrov has left his mark on history through his instinct and an incredibly brave decision; but not just world history, in your life story as well. Because everything was strictly top secret, he was not allowed to tell his wife anything. Instead of receiving a medal of honour, he was reprimanded for not properly recording the incident in the log book.

Our decisions influence our lives and the lives of people around us, often more than we imagine. We underestimate the power they have. Instead, we just nod to ourselves and wonder why nothing ever changes in our lives. We have failed to make a conscious decision to turn a dial or to make a course change.

The thing that impresses me most with Joshua is the biblical report that comes at the end of his life. He calls the people of Israel together at Shechem to remind them of all that God has done for them in the past. Then he challenges them to make a choice: to decide whether they want to follow the old gods of their fathers or serve the one true God. He makes his intentions clear: "My family and I are going to worship and obey the Lord!" (Joshua 24:15, CEV).

This powerful statement and the clear decision are totally inspiring to me. At home, we don't have a Bible verse on every wall, but this particular one hangs by our front door. It is a conscious choice. And our decisions have a mysterious power because God takes them seriously.

That day, all Israel decided to serve the Lord, and Joshua renewed the covenant between them and God. It almost sounds like a gigantic wedding. At the end of this book, only these questions remain: What will you choose? Where exactly would you like to go in your life? Where can New Land become visible in your life? Close this book and make your decision. God will take it seriously and will be with you.

Embrace the Newlandic spirit.

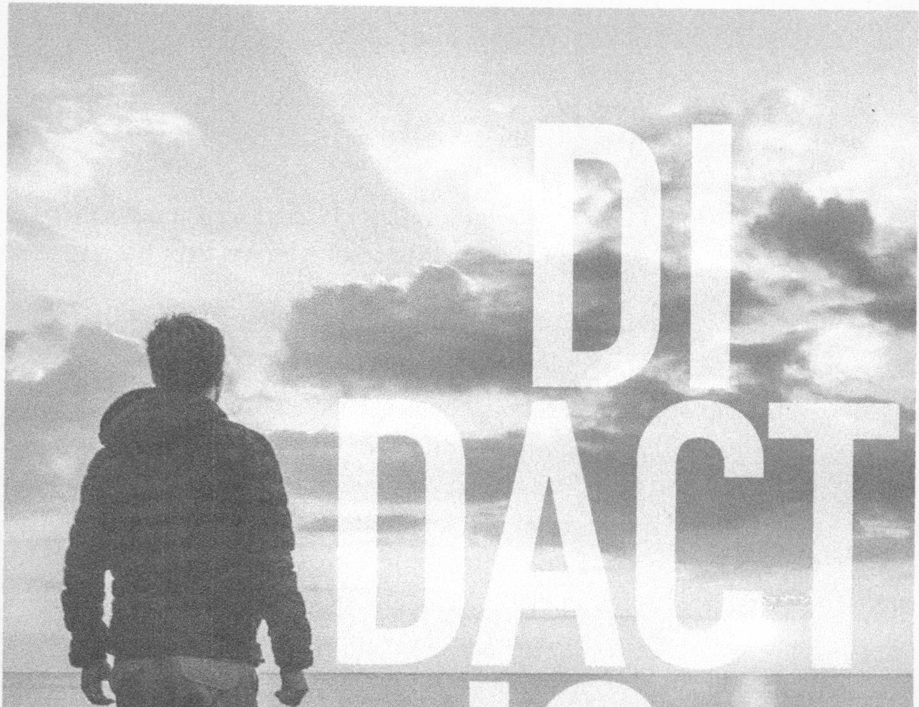
DI
DACT
IC
Notes

1. https://www.nasa.gov/offices/oct/40-years-of-nasa-spinoff (last checked on 4 June 2019).

2. https://youtu.be/W3X-NJFoAdE (last checked on 4 June 2019). The story of Baba Amar Bharati, who has kept his right arm raised since 1973.

3. https://www.sciencedaily.com/releases/2008/02/080207091859.htm or https://www.psychologytoday.com/blog/the-third-age/201405/use-it-or-lose-it (last checked on 4 June 2019

4. Information from https://www.nytimes.com/2011/08/30/science/30species.html (last checked on 4 June 2019).

5. Fritz Rienecker, "Paul's Letter to the Ephesians" ["Der Brief des Paulus an die Epheser"], *Wuppertaler Study Bible* [*Wuppertaler Studienbibel*] (Wuppertal, Germany: Brockhaus, 1994), p. 86.

6. William MacDonald, *Believer's Bible Commentary: New Testament*, 2nd edition (Nashville, Thomas Nelson, 1997). p. 901.

7. From an interview with Richard Kostelanetz, published in Kostelanetz, *Conversing with Cage*, 1st edition (New York: Limelight Editions, 1988).

8. Ulrich Eggers, *Überrascht von Gott* [*Surprised by God*] (Witten, Germany: SCM R.Brockhaus, 2014), p. 16

9. C. G. Jung, *Ein moderner Mythus: Von Dingen, die am Himmel gesehen werden* [*Flying Saucers: A Modern Myth of Things Seen in the Skies*] 1958

10. *Strong's Exhaustive Concordance*, http://biblehub.com/hebrew/3467.htm (last checked on 4 June 2019).

11. Oswald Chambers, *My Utmost for His Highest* (Carnforth, Lancashire: Discovery House Publishers, 2012), p. 259.

12. https://en.wikipedia.org/wiki/As_Slow_as_Possible (last checked on 4 June 2019).

13. Henri J. M. Nouwen, *Was mir am Herzen liegt* [*The Way of the Heart*] (Freiburg im Breisgau, Germany: Herder, 2016), pp. 17–19.

14. Letters 123 and 252. Elizabeth of Dijon.

15. Quote from Meister Eckhart, German mystic and Dominican monk.

16. The calculation: 100,000 hairs grow 1 mm each in three days = 100,000 mm. In one day, one-third or about 33,000 mm = 33 m. In one month that's about 1000 m = 1 km new hair.

17. Rosenthal, R., & Jacobson, L. (1968): *Pygmalion in the classroom: Teacher expectation and pupils' intellectual development*. New York: Holt, Rinehart & Winston

18. https://www.srf.ch/play/radio/mailbox/audio/ verlor-charlie-chaplin-bei-einem-chaplin- doublewettbewerb?id=81e5982d-d0bc-4783-b079- 49a8e3b9140c (last checked on 4 June 2019).

19. Marie von Ebner-Eschenbach, *Aphorismen* (Berlin: Gebrüder Paetel, 1893). English translation from: https:// www.goodreads.com/author/quotes/529837.Marie_von_ Ebner_Eschenbach (last checked on 4 June 2019).

20. https://en.wikipedia.org/wiki/Football_War (last checked on 4 June 2019).

21. https://en.wikipedia.org/wiki/Christmas_truce (last checked on 4 June 2019).

22. https://en.wikipedia.org/wiki/The_Köln_Concert (last checked on 4 June 2019).

23. https://astrosociety.org/edu/publications/tnl/71/howfast. html (last checked on 4 June 2019).

24. https://www.atlasobscura.com/articles/london-is-still-paying-rent-to-the-queen-on-a-property-leased-in-1211 (last checked on 4 June 2019).

25. Raniero Cantalamessa, *Das Antlitz der Barmherzigkeit [The Gaze of Mercy: A Commentary on Divine and Human Mercy (2015)]* (Munich: Neue Stadt, 2016), p. 166.

26. *Ibid.*

27. http://www.neatorama.com/2014/04/28/The-Toilet-that-Sank-the-U-1206/ (last checked on 4 June 2019).

28. https://en.wikipedia.org/wiki/Lazarus_taxon (last checked on 4 June 2019).

29. https://en.wikipedia.org/wiki/Lyall%27s_wren (last checked on 4 June 2019).

30. https://en.wikipedia.org/wiki/Shizo_Kanakuri (last checked on 4 June 2019).

31. https://en.wikipedia.org/wiki/Tree_of_T%C3%A9n%C3%A9r%C3%A9 (last checked on 4 June 2019).

32. C. P. Richter, "On the Phenomenon of Sudden Death in Animals and Men", *Psychosomatic Medicine* 19(3), (May–Jun 1957), pp. 191–98.

33. https://en.wikipedia.org/wiki/Stanislav_Petrov (last checked on 4 June 2019).

"Peter Walker has done the church a great service in this new edition of *The Jesus Way*. It's a remarkable guide – both user-friendly and yet in-depth – as to what it means to follow Jesus today."

Revd Greg Downes, Director of Ministerial Training and Dean of the Wesley Centre for Missional Engagement, Wycliffe Hall, Oxford

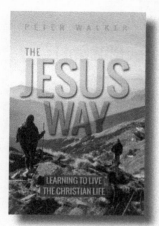

This book teaches the basics of the Christian faith, looking first at what Jesus himself taught, and then at what his apostles had to say. It is for anyone who wants to follow Jesus, but is not sure or would like to be reminded of the way.

In short clear steps, Dr Peter Walker takes us through the basics of enjoying Jesus' forgiveness, welcoming his Spirit and feeding on his scriptures; then explores the principles of worshipping with his people, following his teaching and trusting him with our future.

This second edition has been revised and updated. It can also be used in combination with the brand new *The Jesus Way* courses.

The Jesus Way:
Learning to Live the Christian Life
ISBN: 978 0 85721 960 2 (paperback)
eISBN: 978 0 85721 961 9 (eBook)

Archbishop Benjamin Kwashi is on the front line of faith. Three times terrorists have tried to kill him. Each time they failed to crush his faith or dampen his joy.

Neither bomb nor bullet can silence this priest, who continues to speak truth to power: "Until my time is up, I will live each moment for the gospel, which is the hope of Africa and the world."

Ben Kwashi has been described as one of the most influential Christians alive. His home is in Jos, in Nigeria. Here, Boko Haram and heavily armed Fulani militants are fighting to create a hard-line Islamic state. They have killed thousands and driven millions from their homes.

A brutal assault on his wife Gloria drove Ben to his knees as he made the decision to forgive and found the strength to press on. They have turned their home into an orphanage and its grounds into a zoo.

The challenge of Ben's message – to live joyfully for the gospel, even in the face of terror – has never been so timely. Heart-wrenching and humorous, his story will inspire you to live your life – and your faith – to the full.

Neither Bomb Nor Bullet:
Benjamin Kwashi – Archbishop on the Front Line
ISBN: 987 0 85721 843 8 (paperback)
eISBN: 978 0 85721 844 5 (eBook)

"Gavin and Anne remind us that we have the ability to change the game; not only for us, but also for those we never even get to know this side of heaven."
Christy Wimber, author, speaker, and TV host

"Game Changers is a book for the church in our times."
Rob Parsons OBE, chairman, Care for the Family

Have you ever wanted to change the world?

If you long to see a real and lasting move of God, if you're ready to count the cost and play your part, then Game Changers will inspire and equip you, as you seek to make an impact.

Journey with Moses from the burning bush to the borders of the Promised Land and see how God uses ordinary people to shape a nation.

God is at work in our world today. The question is: do we want to join Him? If so, let's change the game together.

Game Changers:
Encountering God and Changing the World
ISBN: 987 0 85721 926 8 (paperback)
eISBN: 978 0 85721 927 5 (eBook)

"This book is a timely reminder that the highest calling for us as women and men is to the magnificent adventure of pursuing and doing the will of God, whose image we bear."
Rachel Gardner, director at Youthscape, president of Girls' Brigade England & Wales, Home For Good Ambassador

The role of women in church leadership is not a new topic, but one that is still hotly contested. In *Gifted*, Debbie Duncan presents a refreshingly new perspective on how all church leaders can be better at what they do when they listen to the voices of both men and women who lead.

Rooted in Christian tradition, theology, and theory, Debbie Duncan helps us to understand how present-day practices came into being. Testimonials by several women church leaders from a variety of theological backgrounds reflect what is said in each chapter. A book written by a prominent female leader speaking into the lives of other women, and an indispensable resource of encouragement and support for women leaders everywhere.

Gifted:
Women in Leadership
ISBN: 978 0 85721 953 4 (paperback)
eISBN: 978 0 85721 949 7 (eBook)

"I can't think of anyone who has been more effective [than John Stott] in introducing so many people to a biblical worldview. He represents a touchstone of authentic biblical scholarship."
Billy Graham

"Stott's mission is to pierce through all the encrustations and share direct contact with Jesus."
New York Times

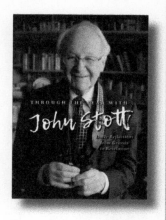

Through the Year with John Stott explores the whole biblical story from creation to the end times in 365 days. One of the most respected Bible teachers of our times, John Stott gets to the heart of each of the 365 carefully selected passages, covering every essential Christian teaching in a single volume. The readings are broken up into weekly themes. Each devotion is based on a key passage of Scripture, and includes biblical references for further exploration.

This new edition includes a new foreword from Old Testament Scholar, Chris Wright.

Through the Year with John Stott:
Daily Reflections from Genesis to Revelation
ISBN: 978 0 85721 962 6 (paperback)
ISBN: 978 0 85721 964 0 (hardback)
eISBN: 978 0 85721 963 3 (eBook)

"The story of the Diospi Suyana hospital is a remarkable example of what can happen when people take God seriously."

John Lennox, Professor of Mathematics, University of Oxford

"A story of medicine, money, and miracles."

Stephen Nolan, Radio Presenter, BBC Radio 5

"You are out of your minds!" That was the reaction of many when they heard that Klaus and Martina John were planning to build a modern hospital for the Peruvian Quechua people without any capital, income, or loans. But the resulting story of Diospi Suyana has become a thriller filled with miracles and examples of divine providence.

Since its inauguration in 2007, the adventure has continued as Diospi Suyana has regularly faced danger, corruption, and seemingly insurmountable obstacles. And yet it continues to grow. The Hospital of Hope has been the subject of 500 media reports around the world.

The unexpected twists and unexplained turns in its history have fascinated millions.

God Has Seen Us:
Diospi Suyana – A Story Shared Around the World
ISBN: 978 0 85721 944 2 (paperback)
eISBN: 978 0 85721 945 9 (eBook)